AS A MATTER OF
COURSE . . .

AS A MATTER OF COURSE . . .

The Mateus Rosé Guide to
Home Entertaining

A Selection of Seasonal menus
prepared by

JENNIE REEKIE

Hutchinson Benham
London

Drawings by Gill Zeiner
Photography by Melvin Grey

Hutchinson Benham Limited
3 Fitzroy Square, London W1P 6JD

An imprint of the Hutchinson Group

London Melbourne Sydney Auckland
Wellington Johannesburg and agencies
throughout the world

First published 1979

Text © Sogrape Ltd 1979
Drawings © Hutchinson Benham Limited 1979

Set in Monophoto Photina

Printed in Italy by A. Mondadori Editore, Verona

British Library Cataloguing in Publication Data

Reekie, Jennie
    As a matter of course.
    1. Cookery
    I. Title
    641.5   TX717

ISBN 0 09 138781 7

CONTENTS

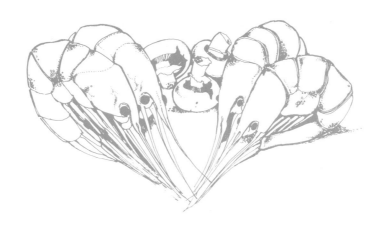

The Palace of Mateus

INTRODUCTION

his is a book of menus for entertaining, from fairly simple lunches and suppers to more elaborate dinner and buffet parties. Although, to a certain extent, seasons for produce have largely disappeared, there are some things that can still only be found at particular times of the year. Most fruit and vegetables are usually at their best and cheapest during their natural season and some fish, especially shellfish, are better at certain times of the year. You will for example always find more crabs at the fishmongers during the summer, whilst mussels still tend to be seen only when there is an R in the month and, unless you freeze it yourself, you will be unable to buy game out of season, even frozen. Generally too it is so much nicer to eat fresh, lighter food in summer than in winter and so for these reasons the menus have all been given a seasonal flavour. To make entertaining more pleasurable, and preparation much simpler, a work plan has been prepared to accompany each menu.

Mateus Rosé has only been made for just over thirty-five years, but the Guedes family in Portugal have been making wine for centuries, mainly the traditional Vinho Verde or green wine of the region. In 1943 Fernando Guedes, who had been educated in England and had worked for a firm of port shippers in London, developed a new wine – a clear pink wine with a slight touch of effervescence or pétillance, as it is also known, made from grapes from the port wine growing area. Fernando developed the idea of the attractively shaped bottle from the local water flagons, and named the wine after the Palace of Mateus, of which there is an illustration on the label of the bottle.

After the war Fernando sent some of his new wine to friends in London and it quickly established itself as an excellent table wine. Travel writers and journalists who visited Portugal wrote glowing reports of it, but in the early 1950s it could only be found on the wine lists of the most exclusive clubs, hotels and restaurants.

The growing popularity of Mateus Rosé then created the need for more and more of the delicious wine in its distinctive bottle, but the Guedes family never wavered from the traditional production method. Every year at harvest time the local people from miles around bring their grapes to the town of Vila Real (or Royal town). From small family vineyards grapes are still brought in,

piled high on the back of mule, donkey or ox carts. The age-old process of pressing the grapes then starts; the juice is allowed to ferment and from this is produced one of the finest blended table wines in the world.

Although Mateus Rosé has been traditionally accepted as the perfect accompaniment to all foods it can also be a delightfully refreshing aperitif. A favourite cocktail is made from mixing a single measure of fine champagne cognac to a glass of chilled Mateus Rosé; with a sharp knife slice a thin sliver of rind from an orange and squeeze it into the wine before dropping the rind into the glass.

SERVING MATEUS ROSÉ

Mateus Rosé must always be served well chilled, and in an ordinary domestic fridge you should allow 3–4 hours to ensure this is done really thoroughly. It can be left for

longer if you wish, so for a lunch party the bottles can be put in the night before, or for dinner or supper they can be put in during the morning, but bottles should not be left in the fridge for several days as this can damage the wine.

If you are short of time, many off-licences now have a chiller from which they sell cold wine and drinks, so first check that there are no ready-chilled bottles there. A quick way to chill the wine is to embed it thoroughly in ice, preferably crushed ice, and then it will only take about thirty minutes.

Do not open the bottle until you are ready to serve the wine or the slight effervescence may be lost. Never use a gas or suction cork remover as there is a danger of the bottle exploding owing to its shape and the effervescence of the wine; always use a conventional corkscrew.

If you have used some of a bottle for cooking, re-cork the bottle tightly and replace in the fridge until required.

QUANTITIES TO ALLOW

For Dinner and Supper Parties:
Allow a third to half a bottle per person, if you are serving aperitifs before the meal, but slightly more if you wish to serve only wine.

For Buffets, Picnics and Barbecues:
Allow a quarter to half a bottle depending on the time of day; people generally drink slightly more in the evening than they do at lunch-time.

For Lunch Parties:
Allow a quarter to a third of a bottle.

PART ONE

LUNCHES

As the majority of people (especially women, who are the people most likely to be entertaining at home at lunch-time) generally prefer a light lunch all the menus, except the Summer Sunday Lunch, consist of just two courses.

All the menus have a fruit-based dessert, chosen because that fruit is in its prime at that time of year; if you possibly can, it is nice to continue this seasonal aspect in the way in which you set the table. If you use a tablecloth you may like to vary this according to the time of year; a light green cloth looks very pretty in spring, a plain or embroidered white one in summer, an orange or brown cloth in autumn, and a rich red one in winter. It is easy too for flower arrangements to continue this theme; crocuses, daffodils or other bulbs for the spring, together with a few catkin, pussy-willow or opening buds. In summer there is a wealth of flowers to choose from, but roses always make very pretty arrangements and are good because they can be put in a low bowl in the centre of the table; wild flowers and grasses can also be used to make a very attractive arrangement. Dahlias and chrysanthemums reflect the autumn colours and are complemented in an arrangement with a few leaves which are just on the turn, while in winter you can use dried flowers.

A good cup of coffee always finishes off a meal well, and at lunch-time people are not worried about the effect of the caffeine keeping them awake at night. There are possibly more different theories on how to make good coffee than days in the year and there are countless different machines available for making coffee, although they all work on similar principles – just steeping the coffee grains in boiling water as in the simple jug method, filtering the coffee through a paper funnel (either from an electric machine or manually), the vacuum method with two bowls which the water and coffee flow between, and the percolator method.

No matter which method you are using, you generally want to allow 2 heaped tablespoons of ground coffee to 6 dl/1 pint water. Whether you grind your own beans or buy ready-ground coffee is a matter of personal choice; the sooner the coffee is used after grinding the better the flavour will be, so only grind as many beans as you require at one time. If you are using bought grounds, keep them in an airtight container and do not buy too large a quantity at once.

Several of the salads in this chapter, and throughout the book, need to be tossed in French dressing, and making a good dressing is very important if you wish to make a good salad. I like to use one part vinegar (either wine or cider vinegar) to three or four parts oil, depending on the salad it is to be used with. The pasta salad on page 16 benefits from extra oil to keep it moist, whereas three parts oil is sufficient for a tossed green salad. The kind of oil you use – olive, corn, sunflower seed, soya bean, etc. – depends largely on the state of your purse (olive oil being much more expensive than the others), and the type of salad you are serving. For a fresh tomato salad I think olive oil is essential, but for a lighter cucumber salad, corn or vegetable oil are quite adequate, although you do want to buy good-quality oil whichever one you are using. As well as the oil and vinegar in the dressing, you should add a little salt, plenty of freshly milled black pepper, a pinch of brown sugar or a little honey if you like your dressing slightly sweet, and a little French mustard. You can also add some crushed garlic and some dried, or finely chopped fresh herbs. French dressing keeps well, so it is a good idea to make a large batch of about 3 dl/½ pint in a screw-topped jar and keep it so that you always have some to hand. Always taste the dressing before adding it to a salad and adjust the seasonings accordingly and it is best to add extra flavourings such as herbs at this stage.

Spring Lunch

∪━━

MENU

Chicken and Asparagus Pancakes
Tossed Green Salad
Rhubarb and Ginger Crunch

[Serves 4–6]

━━∪

A light, simple lunch, with a pleasant feeling of spring about it. If you wish some of the preparation, such as the making of the pancakes and the Rhubarb and Ginger Crunch, can be done the day before, or they can just as easily be made in the morning, according to your plans.

In early spring you will have to use canned or frozen asparagus for the pancakes, but in the late spring the first of the home-grown asparagus starts to arrive in the shops and this is a good way of making a little go quite a long way. Rhubarb is always a good buy at this time of year as it is one of the few fruits readily available at a reasonable price, and the addition of a little chopped crystallized or preserved ginger gives it an interesting flavour.

Chicken and Asparagus Pancakes

For the pancakes
100 g/4 oz. flour
pinch salt
1 egg
3 dl/½ pint milk
2 tablespoons melted butter
oil for frying

For the filling
½ chicken, weighing 650 g/1½ lb. approx.
1 onion, peeled and chopped
rind ½ lemon
sprig thyme
salt
½ teaspoon peppercorns
6 dl/1 pint water
340 g/12 oz. can asparagus spears or 225 g/8 oz.
frozen or fresh asparagus
65 g/2½ oz. butter
50 g/2 oz. flour

Sift together the flour and salt. Add the egg and half the milk and beat until smooth, then gradually beat in the remaining milk and the butter. Use the mixture to make about 12 pancakes, separating each one with a piece of greaseproof paper.

Put the chicken into a pan with the onion, lemon rind, thyme, salt and peppercorns. Pour over the water and bring to the boil. Remove any scum, then cover and simmer gently for 45 minutes or until the chicken is very tender. Remove from the heat and cool enough to handle. Remove the chicken from the cooking liquor and cut the flesh into 1.5 cm/½ inch pieces, discarding the skin and bone. Strain off the liquor from canned asparagus and make up to 6 dl/1 pint with the liquor from cooking the chicken; if using frozen or fresh asparagus cook in boiling salted water until tender and take 3 dl/½ pint asparagus cooking liquor, again making it up to 6 dl/1 pint with chicken stock. Chop the asparagus, reserving a few spears for garnish. Melt 50 g/2 oz. of the butter in a pan. Add the flour and cook for a minute, then gradually stir in the chicken and asparagus stock and bring to the boil, stirring all the time. Add the chicken and asparagus, then taste and adjust the seasoning. Remove from the heat and allow to cool slightly. Put a spoonful of this stuffing into each pancake, roll up and place in an ovenproof dish. Melt the remaining butter and brush all over the top of the pancakes. Cover and cook in a moderately hot oven, 190 °C/375 °F., Gas Mark 5, for 40 minutes. Garnish with the reserved asparagus spears before serving.

Rhubarb and Ginger Crunch

50 g/2 oz. soft brown sugar
25 g/1 oz. butter
1 tablespoon golden syrup
75 g/3 oz. rolled oats
450 g/1 lb. rhubarb
75 g/3 oz. granulated sugar
1 tablespoon water
1.5 dl/¼ pint double cream
25 g/1 oz. crystallized or preserved ginger

To decorate
4–6 slices orange

Put the brown sugar, butter and syrup into a pan, and heat gently until the butter has melted and the sugar dissolved. Remove from the heat and stir in the oats. Press into a 17.5 cm/7 inch sandwich tin and bake in a

Work Plan

The day before or early in the morning
★ Put Mateus Rosé into fridge to chill.
★ Prepare pancakes and chicken and asparagus sauce.
★ Prepare crunch and rhubarb mixture.

One hour before serving
★ Assemble Chicken and Asparagus Pancakes ready to put in oven 40 minutes before serving.
★ Wash and prepare salad – toss in dressing just before serving.
★ Complete Rhubarb and Ginger Crunch.

moderate oven, 180 °C/350 °F., Gas Mark 4, for 15–20 minutes or until golden brown. Remove from the oven and allow to cool in the tin. When cold, remove from tin and break into pieces with your fingers. Cut the rhubarb into 5 cm/2 inch lengths. Put into a pan with the granulated sugar and water, cover and cook over a gentle heat until soft. Allow to cool, then sieve or purée in a blender. Whip the cream until stiff and finely chop the ginger, then fold them both into the cold rhubarb. Divide between 4–6 glasses and chill. Shortly before serving, sprinkle over the crumbled oat mixture and decorate each glass with a twist of orange.

Note: The quantity of oatmeal mixture is fairly generous, so if you are only serving 4 people you may wish to use only two-thirds of this with the whole quantity of rhubarb.

Autumn Lunch

MENU

Pork and Peppers
Boiled Noodles or Sauté Potatoes
Marmalade and Apple Flan

[Serves 4]

Work Plan

The day before or early in the morning
★ Put Mateus Rosé into fridge to chill.
★ Prepare Marmalade and Apple Flan.
★ Par-boil potatoes if using.

Before serving
★ Prepare and cook pork 30 minutes before serving.
★ Cook noodles or potatoes just before serving.

Pork and Peppers

25 g/1 oz. butter
2 tablespoons oil
4 pork chops, each about 225 g/8 oz.
1 medium-sized onion, peeled and chopped
1 small clove garlic, crushed (optional)
2 green peppers, de-seeded and sliced
2 red peppers, de-seeded and sliced
225 g/8 oz. tomatoes, peeled and chopped
3 tablespoons Mateus Rosé
1 teaspoon chopped fresh sage or good pinch dried sage
salt and freshly milled black pepper

Heat the butter and oil in a large frying pan. Add the chops to the pan and cook quickly on either side until browned. Remove from the pan and put on one side. Add the onion and garlic to the fat remaining in the pan and fry gently for 5 minutes. Add the peppers and cook gently for a further 5 minutes; then add the tomatoes, Mateus Rosé, sage and seasoning. Replace the chops in the pan, cover the pan and simmer gently for a further 20 minutes or until the chops are very tender.

Marmalade and Apple Flan

For the pastry
150 g/6 oz. flour
pinch salt
75 g/3 oz. butter or margarine
about 2 tablespoons water

For the filling
650 g/1½ lb. cooking apples
4 tablespoons marmalade
2 teaspoons water

Sift together the flour and salt. Rub in the fat until the mixture resembles fine breadcrumbs, then bind with the water to make a firm dough. Turn on to a floured surface, knead lightly, then roll out and use to line a 20 cm/8 inch flan dish or tin. Fill the centre with greaseproof paper and baking beans and bake in a moderately hot oven, 200 °C/400 °F., Gas Mark 6, for 10 minutes. Remove the greaseproof paper and beans, and bake for a further 5 minutes to dry out the base.

While the pastry is cooking, peel, core and thinly slice the apples. Spread a third of the marmalade over the base of the flan dish, cover with half the apple slices, then spread with half the remaining marmalade. Cover with the last of the apples, arranged attractively on the top. Replace in the oven and cook for 35 minutes or until the apples are quite tender. Put the remaining marmalade into a small pan with the water and heat gently until the marmalade has melted, then boil for 1 minute. Remove from the heat. Remove the flan from the oven and while still hot, brush all over the apples with the warm marmalade glaze.

Winter Lunch

⌒—

MENU

Mixed Fish Pie
Spinach or Broccoli
Tangerine Ice Cream

[Serves 4]

—⌒

Mixed Fish Pie

225 g/8 oz. white fish – cod, haddock, etc.
4 scallops
1 small onion, peeled and chopped
a good pinch dried mixed herbs
peeled rind ½ lemon
salt and freshly milled black pepper
1.5 dl/¼ pint Mateus Rosé
50 g/2 oz. butter
50 g/2 oz. flour
1.5 dl/¼ pint milk
50 g/2 oz. button mushrooms, sliced
100 g/4 oz. prawns
370 g/13 oz. packet frozen puff pastry, thawed
a little beaten egg to glaze

Put the white fish, scallops, onion, mixed herbs, lemon rind and seasoning into a small pan. Pour over the Mateus Rosé and bring just to boiling point. Remove from the heat and allow to cool, then drain, reserving the cooking liquor. Chop the scallops into 1.5 cm/½ inch pieces and flake the white fish. Melt the butter in a clean pan, add the flour and cook for a minute. Gradually stir in the milk and reserved cooking liquor and bring to the boil, stirring all the time. Add the mushrooms and cook gently for 2–3 minutes, then remove from the heat, stir in the white fish, scallops and prawns and taste and adjust the seasoning. Allow to cool.

Roll out the pastry and cut into two rectangles, each 30 × 20 cm/12 × 8 inches. Place the filling on one piece of pastry on a baking tray, and spread to within 1.5 cm/½ inch of the edge. Brush the edge with beaten egg, place the second piece of pastry on top and seal the edges. Using the back of a knife, mark the pastry into diamonds, then brush all over with beaten egg. Bake in a hot oven, 220 °C/425 °F., Gas Mark 7, for 30 minutes or until golden brown.

Work Plan

The day before
★ Make Tangerine Ice Cream. Store in freezer until 10 minutes before serving.

Early in the morning
★ Put Mateus Rosé into fridge to chill.
★ Make fish pie, cover and put in fridge until ready to bake.
★ Prepare vegetables.

Before serving
★ Put fish pie into oven 30 minutes before serving.
★ Cook vegetables just before serving.

Tangerine Ice Cream

3 egg yolks
finely grated rind and juice 4 tangerines,
Wilkins or Satsumas
75 g/3 oz. sugar
1.5 dl/¼ pint single cream
1.5 dl/¼ pint double cream

Beat the egg yolks with the rind in a large bowl. Make the juice from the tangerines up to 1.5 dl/¼ pint with water. Put into a saucepan with the sugar and put over a low heat until the sugar has melted; then boil rapidly until a little of the sugar put into a basin of cold water forms a thread. Remove from the heat and allow to cool for a minute. then slowly whisk into the egg yolks and continue whisking until a mousse-like consistency is formed. Whisk the single and double cream together until thick, then fold in the tangerine mixture. Put into a freezer and freeze until almost firm, then remove from the freezer and beat again until smooth. Pack into a suitable container and freeze for 4 hours until firm.

Summer Sunday Lunch

MENU

Iced Courgette Soup
Cold Roast Pork with Tonnato Sauce
Pasta and Pepper Salad
French Cucumber Salad
Tomato and Watercress Salad
Frosty Raspberry Dessert
Mateus Wine Cup

[Serves 10–12]

Sunday lunch is usually a family occasion, but feeding both adults and young children can be a problem if you wish to produce interesting food for the adults, but also food which the children will eat, so this menu has been designed with this in mind for 6 adults and 4–6 children. Starting backwards, I find the pudding just as popular with children as it is with adults; an American recipe,

it is similar to an ice cream, but the high sugar content prevents it from freezing very firmly and it is best served when half-frozen. For the main course, only cover two-thirds of the pork with the tonnato sauce and simply serve the remainder for the children as cold pork with mayonnaise or salad dressing. They can then either have a little of the adults' salads, or simply have some straight pieces of lettuce, tomato and cucumber which is no extra bother, and they can also be given plenty of fresh bread to help fill them up. As most children are quite happy just eating two courses I have not included them for the soup, but you could always give them all a small cup of tomato juice so that they do not feel left out; nor of course is the wine cup intended for them.

Work Plan

The day before

★ Make the soup, cover and put into fridge to chill.

★ Roast the pork, arrange on the serving dish with the Tonnato Sauce, cover and put into the fridge.

★ Make the Frosty Raspberry Dessert and put into the freezer.

★ Put Mateus Rosé and lemonade in fridge to chill.

In the morning

★ Prepare all the salads.

★ Make wine cup 1 hour before serving.

Iced Courgette Soup

50 g/2 oz. butter
450 g/1 lb. Spanish onions, peeled and chopped
900 g/2 lb. courgettes, sliced
3 cloves garlic, crushed
3 dl/$\frac{1}{2}$ pint stock
salt and freshly milled black pepper

To garnish
1 courgette, sliced

Melt the butter in a large pan. Add the onions and fry gently for 5 minutes; then add the courgettes, toss lightly in the butter, cover and simmer gently for 45 minutes. Remove from the heat and allow to cool, then sieve or purée in a blender. Add the garlic and stock, and season with salt and plenty of freshly milled black pepper. Chill for several hours before serving, garnished with fresh sliced courgette.

Pork with Tonnato Sauce

2.25 kg/5 lb. leg of pork, boned
juice 1 lemon
salt and freshly milled black pepper
1 sprig sage

For the sauce
198 g/7 oz. can tuna in oil
3 dl/$\frac{1}{2}$ pint mayonnaise
juice $\frac{1}{2}$ lemon
50 g/1$\frac{3}{4}$ oz. can anchovy fillets
1 tablespoon chopped capers
salt and freshly milled black pepper
about 6 tablespoons pork, veal or chicken stock

To garnish
1 teaspoon capers
8–10 lemon wedges

Bone the pork or ask the butcher to do this for you. Tie into a neat joint with string and place in a roasting tin. Place the sprig of sage under the joint, season with salt and pepper and pour over the lemon juice. Roast in a moderately hot oven, 190 °C/375 °F., Gas Mark 5, for 1$\frac{3}{4}$ hours. Remove from the oven and allow to cool, then cut into thin slices and arrange on a serving plate. (Any slices for children which you do not want covered with sauce should be put on a separate serving dish.)

Finely mash the tuna together with the oil from the can. Stir in the mayonnaise and lemon juice. Finely chop half the anchovies, reserving the remainder for garnishing. Add to the tuna mixture with the capers, and season to taste with salt and pepper. Add just enough cold stock to give the sauce the consistency of thick cream, then pour over the pork. Cover and chill for up to 12 hours. Before serving, garnish with the remainder of the anchovy fillets, cut in half lengthways, the capers and lemon wedges.

French Cucumber Salad

Thinly peel a large cucumber. Slice very thinly, put into a colander and sprinkle with 1 teaspoon salt, preferably sea salt. Leave to drain for 30 minutes, then dry thoroughly. Place in a serving dish, pour over 2 table-spoons French dressing, toss lightly and sprinkle liberally with chopped parsley before serving.

Pasta and Pepper Salad

Cook 225 g/8 oz. pasta shapes in boiling salted water until just tender. Drain, rinse in cold water and drain thoroughly again. Toss with 4 tablespoons French dressing, and a clove crushed garlic (if wished) while still warm, then allow to cool. Dice a red and a green pepper, discarding the cores and seeds. Add to the pasta with 3 sticks chopped celery, plenty of salt and freshly milled black pepper, and toss lightly together.

Tomato and Watercress Salad

Trim off the stalks from a large bunch of watercress. Wash and dry thoroughly and put into a salad bowl. Peel and thinly slice ½ large Spanish onion and cut 450–650 g/1–1½ lb. tomatoes into quarters. Add to the watercress in the bowl and sprinkle with 1 tablespoon sunflower seeds. Just before serving, pour over 3 table-spoons French dressing and toss lightly together.

Frosty Raspberry Dessert

For the crumb mixture
150 g/6 oz. plain flour
75 g/3 oz. soft brown sugar
50 g/2 oz. walnuts, almonds or hazelnuts, chopped
100 g/4 oz. butter, melted

For the raspberry mixture
2 egg whites
2 tablespoons lemon juice
450 g/1 lb. fresh or frozen raspberries, defrosted
225 g/8 oz. caster sugar
1.5 dl/¼ pint double cream
1.5 dl/¼ pint single cream

Sift the flour into a bowl. Add the sugar, nuts and butter, and mix together. Spread evenly over the base of a 17.5 × 27.5 cm/7 × 11 inch Swiss roll tin and bake in a moderate oven, 180 °C/350 °F., Gas Mark 4, for 20 minutes. Remove from the oven and allow to cool; then with your fingers break into crumbs. Put the egg whites, lemon juice and most of the raspberries (reserving some for decoration) into a large bowl. Whisk gently together with an electric mixer then gradually whisk in the sugar. Beat at a high speed for about 10 minutes or until the mixture forms stiff peaks. Whip the single and double cream together until stiff, then fold into the raspberry mixture. Spoon half the raspberry mixture into the base of a large dish (plastic, perspex or other suitable dish which will withstand freezing). Sprinkle over half the crumbs, then spoon in the remainder of the raspberry mixture and top with the last of the crumbs. Put into a freezer and freeze for at least 6 hours. Decorate with the remaining raspberries before serving.

Mateus Wine Cup

2 bottles Mateus Rosé
9 dl/1½ pints lemonade
1.5 dl/¼ pint cheap brandy
2 oranges, sliced
2 bananas, peeled and sliced
2 apples, cored and chopped
225 g/8 oz. grapes

Chill Mateus Rosé and lemonade for at least 4 hours. Pour the wine and brandy into a bowl or jug and add all the fruit. Leave to marinate in the fridge for about 1 hour. Pour in the lemonade just before serving and stir well.

PART TWO
SUPPERS

Suppers are generally rather informal occasions when you invite friends round for a fairly simple meal, and these menus have mostly been kept just to two courses to serve either four or six people.

In the Spring Menu on page 20, rather than serving a dessert, I have suggested serving a pâté followed by a veal casserole and then fruit and cheese; you could of course serve fruit and cheese instead of, or as well as, a dessert in the other menus. In summer especially there are so many delicious fruits around, and they can look so attractive arranged in a fruit bowl that sometimes it seems quite unnecessary to go to the bother of making a dessert – and it is better for the waist-line. Some of the more exotic fruits, such as mangoes, pawpaws, passion fruit, guavas, can now be found in local supermarkets and greengrocers and not just in exclusive London shops, so if you are feeling extravagant, lash out and buy some of these, as well as the more usual apples, pears, bananas, grapes, etc.

Almost all fresh fruit bruises fairly easily, so you need to treat it gently; wash carefully and dry on soft kitchen paper. Hard fruit, such as apples and pears, also benefits from a little gentle polishing to bring up the shine. Any fruit which is unripe when you buy it will ripen quicker if it is put into the bowl with other fruit.

When it comes to cheeseboards, if you are only having four or six people for supper you do not want to buy a wide variety of different cheeses; a couple is quite adequate. Choose one hard and one soft cheese, or one hard cheese, such as an English Farmhouse Cheddar or Double Gloucester, and a blue cheese, such as Stilton or Gorgonzola. It is also best not to buy too large a quantity as many cheeses deteriorate once a piece has been cut off the main cheese; if you allow 100 g/4 oz.

per person that should be plenty.

Provided you can store them in a cool place, the majority of cheeses are best not kept in the fridge, especially if you are only keeping them for a day or two. Wrap them first in greaseproof paper and then in a piece of muslin or a clean tea towel and put in a cool place. However, should you buy a Brie or Camembert, for example, which is slightly under-ripe, you should leave it in a warm place if you wish to speed up the ripening process.

Making a cheeseboard look attractive need only take a few minutes, but makes the cheese look so much more appetizing. The simplest garnish of all is some sprigs of parsley or watercress, but you can also use a few radishes or spring onions, little sticks of celery or bunches of grapes, or arrange the cheese on vine or other suitable leaves, if you have them.

As suppers are often a time when you entertain close friends, they are an ideal opportunity to experiment with new dishes; if you are a little worried about serving some of the more elaborate dinner party dishes on pages 30–44 you could make them up for supper, just to try them out. Equally, once you have made up some of the recipes in this chapter (I always think it is advisable to make up a recipe once according to the instructions before you try your own variation), you can try adding subtle changes of flavour. For example, the Spicy Curried Lamb on page 25 has a high proportion of coriander seed in it; you might like to try reducing this and increasing the amount of cumin and/or adding a teaspoon or two of ground turmeric. In the Casseroled Veal with Black Olives on page 20 you could try replacing the marjoram with tarragon, but only use half as much tarragon as it has a stronger, and more distinctive, flavour than marjoram.

After-The-Show Supper

for Autumn or Winter

MENU

Eggs Aurore
Middle Eastern Casserole
Boiled Rice
Chocolate and Chestnut Log

[Serves 6]

Entertaining after you have been out in the evening, whether it is to a theatre, cinema, concert or even the children's school play, can be a headache for the hostess. This menu consists of a cold starter and dessert, both of which can be completely prepared in advance and left in the fridge, and a main course which cooks very slowly in a low oven for hours; all you have to do when you come in is to boil some rice. The Eastern Mediterranean countries abound with recipes for dishes which are cooked very slowly overnight, and it is an excellent way of cooking to ensure that the meat is very tender and you have the maximum flavour from it.

Chestnuts make marvellous autumn and winter desserts and although I have suggested using a can of chestnut purée here to save time, you could of course make your own chestnut purée from fresh ones if you preferred. Make a slit in the nuts and boil for about 10 minutes. Drain, peel and cook in a little milk until tender. Drain and purée.

Eggs Aurore

6 eggs
1.5 dl/$\frac{1}{4}$ pint soured cream
1.5 dl/$\frac{1}{4}$ pint mayonnaise
1 tablespoon tomato ketchup
a few drops Tabasco
2 teaspoons chopped gherkins
1 tablespoon chopped parsley
$\frac{1}{2}$ small red pepper, de-seeded and finely diced
1 tablespoon chopped parsley
1 teaspoon chopped capers
salt and freshly milled black pepper

To garnish
watercress

Hard-boil the eggs for 10 minutes, plunge into cold water, then shell and cut in half lengthways, and arrange on one large or individual serving plates. Mix the cream with the mayonnaise, tomato ketchup, Tabasco, gherkins, parsley, red pepper, and capers. Season to taste with salt and plenty of freshly milled black pepper. Spoon over the eggs, then cover with cling-wrap and place in the fridge. Before serving, remove the cling-wrap and garnish with watercress.

Middle Eastern Casserole

2 lean necks English lamb, each weighing about
1.25 kg/2½ lb.
2 tablespoons oil
450 g/1 lb. onions, peeled and chopped
2 cloves garlic, crushed
1 teaspoon ground coriander
1 teaspoon dried mixed herbs
142 g/5 oz. can tomato purée
9 dl/1½ pints water
450 g/1 lb. frozen peas

Ask the butcher to cut each neck into 3 pieces. Remove any excess fat and all the sinews. Heat the oil in a large frying pan and quickly fry the meat on all sides until browned. Remove from the pan and place in a casserole. Add the onions, garlic, coriander and herbs and fry gently in the fat remaining for 10 minutes. Stir in the tomato purée and water, stir well, season and bring to the boil. Pour over the meat in the casserole, cover the casserole and cook in a very low oven, 120 °C/250 °F., Gas Mark ½, for eight hours. Stir in the frozen peas, return to the oven and cook for a further 20 minutes. Taste and adjust the seasoning before serving.

Chocolate and Chestnut Log

3 eggs
75 g/3 oz. caster sugar
½ teaspoon vanilla essence
50 g/2 oz. self-raising flour
pinch of salt
25 g/1 oz. cocoa powder
440 g/15½ oz. can chestnut purée
50 g/2 oz. soft brown sugar
2 tablespoons rum
milk (see method)
50 g/2 oz. plain chocolate
1.5 dl/¼ pint double cream
2 tablespoons single cream

Grease and line a 32.5 × 22.5 cm/13 × 9 inch Swiss roll tin with greased greaseproof or silicone paper. Whisk the eggs and caster sugar together until it is thick and creamy and the whisk leaves a trail when lifted out of the mixture. Sift in the flour, salt and cocoa and carefully fold into the mixture.

Turn into the prepared tin, level off and bake in a moderately hot oven, 200 °C/400 °F., Gas Mark 6, for about 12 minutes or until the mixture springs back when lightly pressed. Turn out on to a piece of greaseproof paper, dredged with icing or caster sugar, trim off the edges, then roll up with the greaseproof paper. Put on one side and allow to cool.

Beat the chestnut purée with the brown sugar and rum to give a soft spreading consistency; if the mixture is still too stiff add a little milk. Pare the chocolate with a potato peeler to make curls and whip the double and single cream together until stiff.

Unroll the Swiss roll, spread over 3 tablespoons of the whipped cream, then the chestnut purée then sprinkle over half the chocolate curls. Re-roll the Swiss roll and place on a serving dish. Spread the rest of the cream all over the top and sides of the cake, and draw a fork lightly through it along the length of the log to give a bark-like effect. Make a foil 'tent' to cover the log lightly and chill in the fridge until ready to serve.

Remove the foil tent and sprinkle the log with the remainder of the chocolate curls just before serving.

Spring Supper

MENU

Easy Liver Pâté
Casseroled Veal with Black Olives
New Potatoes
Buttered Peas and Cucumber
Cheese and Fresh Fruit

[Serves 6]

Pâté is always a popular starter for a meal and has the added advantage that it can be made several days in advance, provided it is sealed with butter.

A veal casserole makes a pleasant change from the more usual beef, lamb or chicken, but if you have difficulty in obtaining veal, you could use pork instead which will give you an equally delicious result. I suggest making it earlier in the day and reheating, but do not add the cream and olives until just before serving.

The spring can be a difficult time of year for fresh vegetables, but frozen peas with some chopped cucumber added makes an interesting vegetable dish.

Easy Liver Pâté

75 g/3 oz. butter
1 small onion, peeled and finely chopped
1 clove garlic, crushed
1 sprig thyme or $\frac{1}{2}$ teaspoon dried thyme
100 g/4 oz. streaky or flank bacon
100 g/4 oz. pig's liver
225 g/8 oz. chickens' livers
1$\frac{1}{2}$ tablespoons brandy
salt and freshly milled black pepper

Melt 25 g/1 oz. of the butter in a large frying pan and gently fry the onion and garlic with the thyme for 5 minutes. Cut off the rind from the bacon and chop the bacon roughly. Add to the pan and fry for a further 5 minutes. Roughly chop the pig's liver and add to the pan with the chickens' livers. Cook over a very gentle heat for about 10 minutes, then remove from the heat and purée until smooth. Cream 25 g/1 oz. of the

Work Plan

The day before or earlier
★ Make pâté.

In the afternoon
★ Put Mateus Rosé into fridge to chill.
★ Prepare and cook veal casserole.
★ Prepare cheeseboard, cover and put in a cool place.
★ Prepare potatoes.
★ Prepare fruit bowl.

Before serving
★ Reheat casserole for 30 minutes before serving.
★ Cook vegetables just before serving.

remaining butter and add to the mixture with the brandy. Season to taste and pack into a container. Melt the remaining butter and pour over the top.

Casseroled Veal with Black Olives

650 g/1$\frac{1}{2}$ lb. stewing veal
50 g/2 oz. butter
1 tablespoon oil
2 medium-sized onions, peeled and finely chopped
50 g/2 oz. flour
1.5 dl/$\frac{1}{4}$ pint Mateus Rosé
3 dl/$\frac{1}{2}$ pint veal or chicken stock
juice 1 lemon
450 g/1 lb. young carrots, scraped and sliced
1 teaspoon dried marjoram
salt and freshly milled black pepper
50 g/2 oz. black olives
1.5 dl/$\frac{1}{4}$ pint soured cream

Cut the meat into 2.5 cm/1 inch cubes. Heat the butter and oil in a pan and gently fry the onions for 5 minutes. Add the meat and cook until the sides of the meat are sealed, but not browned. Stir in the flour and cook for 2 minutes, stirring, then gradually stir in the Mateus Rosé, veal or chicken stock and lemon juice. Bring to the boil, stirring all the time. Add the carrots, marjoram and seasoning, cover the pan and simmer gently for 1$\frac{1}{4}$ hours. Stir in the olives and cream and heat gently without allowing the sauce to boil.

Buttered Peas and Cucumber

Melt 50 g/2 oz. butter in a pan and gently fry a small chopped onion for 5 minutes until soft but not coloured. Add half a diced cucumber and cook gently for a further 2 minutes, then add 450 g/1 lb. frozen peas, a good pinch dried mint, salt and freshly milled black pepper. Cover the pan and simmer gently for 15 minutes or until the peas are quite tender.

Spring Supper

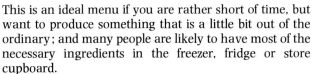

MENU

*French-Style Roast Chicken
with Ham and Mushrooms
Roast Potatoes
Leeks
Quick Caribbean Fool*

[Serves 4]

This is an ideal menu if you are rather short of time, but want to produce something that is a little bit out of the ordinary; and many people are likely to have most of the necessary ingredients in the freezer, fridge or store cupboard.

The Lyons area of France is particularly well known for the way in which they stuff chickens between the skin and the flesh of the bird and this makes the bird extremely succulent, as well as adding plenty of flavour to some of the rather tasteless birds we have these days. It is not difficult to do and once the chicken and potatoes have been prepared they can be left to roast in the oven and require no extra attention. It is best to cut the potatoes into fairly small pieces, about 7.5 cm/3 inches, so that they require the same cooking time as the chicken and if they are par-boiled for 5 minutes first, you will achieve a crisper result. Put the potatoes into a roasting tin above the chicken for half the cooking time, then transfer them to the bottom so that the skin of the chicken can become golden brown.

French-Style Roast Chicken with Ham and Mushrooms

1 roasting chicken, about 1.25 kg/3 lb.
75 g/3 oz. butter
2 tablespoons chopped parsley
1 small clove garlic, crushed (optional)
salt and freshly milled black pepper
4 slices cooked ham (150 g/6 oz. approx.)
100 g/4 oz. button mushrooms
peeled rind ½ lemon
a pinch dried thyme

Loosen the skin of the chicken over the breast and legs so that you can put your hand between the skin and the flesh. Beat 50 g/2 oz. of the butter, then beat in the parsley, garlic if using, salt and plenty of pepper. Spread half of this butter on the flesh of the bird under the skin and spread the remainder on the slices of ham. Lay two slices of ham (butter side up) between the flesh and the skin over the breast and one slice over each leg. Clean the mushrooms, but leave them whole and put into a bowl. Cut the remaining butter into small pieces and add to the mushrooms with the lemon rind, thyme and seasoning. Toss lightly together and use this mixture to stuff the bird. Season the outside of the bird with salt and pepper. Roast in a moderately hot oven, 190 °C/375 °F., Gas Mark 5, for 1¼ hours.

Quick Caribbean Fool

3 ripe bananas
226 g/8 oz. can pineapple pieces
1–2 tablespoons rum
2 tablespoons chopped nuts
1 tablespoon mixed candied peel

Put the bananas into a blender together with the juice from the canned pineapple. Blend until a smooth purée. Reserve 4 pineapple pieces for decoration, add the remainder to the bananas and blend for a few seconds more so that they are slightly broken up; the pineapple should not be completely smooth. Pour into a bowl, stir in the rum, nuts and peel. Pour into 4 small glasses, top each one with a reserved piece of pineapple and chill.

21

Summer Supper

MENU

*Baked Fish with Dill
and Cucumber Sauce
Mange Tout Peas
New Potatoes with Chopped
Parsley
Port and Cherry Compôte*

[Serves 6]

Fish makes a very pleasant light summer supper, especially in hot weather. This recipe makes use of steaks of white fish and is served with a sauce more commonly reserved for salmon, which makes the white fish just a little bit 'special'. It is a variation of a Hollandaise sauce with chopped cooked cucumber added to it and plenty of dill; ideally use fresh dill but you can perfectly well use dried, but remember it is the green 'weed', as it is known, you are using and not the seed. Fresh dill is not easy to buy in shops, but it is not difficult to grow yourself, and its slightly aniseed flavour enhances many fish and meat dishes as well as salads.

Fresh cherries, although delicious eaten *au naturel* also make an excellent compôte and if you are lucky enough to have, or are able to buy some fresh Morello cherries it will taste even better, but in that case you will need a little extra sugar.

23

Baked Fish with Dill and Cucumber Sauce

6 steaks, each weighing about 225 g/8 oz.
of haddock, halibut, turbot, cod, etc.
peeled rind and juice 1 small lemon
1 onion, peeled and sliced
4 tablespoons Mateus Rosé
salt and freshly milled black pepper
1 cucumber
150 g/6 oz. butter, preferably unsalted
3 egg yolks
2 tablespoons chopped fresh or 2 teaspoons dried dill
1 teaspoon fresh or $\frac{1}{4}$ teaspoon dried tarragon
1 tablespoon chopped parsley

To garnish
few sprigs fresh dill

Put the steaks into an ovenproof dish with the lemon rind, onion, wine and plenty of seasoning. Cover and cook in a moderately hot oven, 200 °C/400 °F., Gas Mark 6, for 30 minutes. Peel the cucumber and cut into 0.75 cm/$\frac{1}{4}$ inch dice. Melt 25 g/1 oz. of the butter, add the cucumber and seasoning, cover and cook gently for 10 minutes. Remove from the heat. Beat the egg yolks with the lemon juice and 25 g/1 oz. of the softened butter in a basin, or the top of a double saucepan, placed over a pan of gently simmering water; it is important that the water is not boiling rapidly or the sauce will curdle. Gradually beat in the remainder of the butter a dessertspoon at a time, beating well between each addition. Add the dill, tarragon and parsley, then half the cooked cucumber. Remove the fish from the oven, place on a heated serving dish and garnish with the remaining cooked cucumber and a few sprigs of fresh dill. Strain all the cooking liquor and add about 5 tablespoons to the sauce. Taste, adjust seasoning and serve separately with the fish.

Port and Cherry Compôte

650 g/1$\frac{1}{2}$ lb. cherries, preferably dark red ones
1.5 dl/$\frac{1}{4}$ pint water
2 tablespoons granulated sugar
grated rind and juice 1 large orange
3 tablespoons redcurrant jelly
pinch of ground cinnamon
4 tablespoons port
2 tablespoons flaked almonds (optional)

Stone the cherries, or leave them whole if short of time. Put the water, sugar, orange rind and juice, redcurrant jelly and cinnamon into a pan and heat gently until the sugar has dissolved and the jelly melted. Add the cherries and poach gently for 15 minutes. Remove from the heat, stir in the port, then cool and chill until ready to serve. If liked a few flaked almonds can be sprinkled on the top before serving.

Autumn Supper

MENU

Spicy Curried Lamb
Boiled Rice
Poppadums
Danish Plum Layer

[Serves 4]

Although the Indians of course eat their hot curries in a hot climate, we generally tend to eat them during the colder months; this is an ideal menu for the days when the first autumn nip is in the air, but there is still a plentiful supply of fresh plums around to make the dessert (although you could always use frozen plums when fresh are unavailable).

This recipe is not for a hot curry, but for a mild spicy curry and it can be served with a variety of different accompaniments, as well as boiled rice and poppadums, such as mango chutney, finely chopped raw onion, finely chopped red and green peppers, chopped tomatoes etc.

The Danish Plum Layer is an adaptation of a famous Danish recipe for layered apple, known by the attractive name of Peasant Girl with Veil, although which part is the peasant and which the veil I have never been able to discover!

Work Plan

Earlier in the day
★ **Put Mateus Rosé into fridge to chill.**
★ **Prepare Danish Plum Layer.**

In the afternoon
★ **Prepare curry and leave to cook.**
★ **Prepare tray of accompaniments and cover.**

Before serving
★ **Cook rice and poppadums just before serving.**

Spicy Curried Lamb

650 g/1½ lb. lean lamb; use fillet, shoulder or leg
25 g/1 oz. desiccated coconut
1.5 dl/¼ pint boiling water
50 g/2 oz. butter
2 onions, peeled and chopped
2 cloves garlic, crushed
1 teaspoon powdered ginger
2 teaspoons coriander seeds
½ teaspoon ground turmeric
½–1 teaspoon chilli powder
1 teaspoon ground cumin
1½ teaspoons garam masala
56 g/2¼ oz. can concentrated tomato purée
salt

Cut the meat into 2.5 cm/1 inch cubes. Put the coconut into a jug, pour over the boiling water and leave for 10 minutes. Heat the butter in a large pan and gently fry the meat with the onions, garlic and all the spices for about 10 minutes, stirring well. Add the tomato purée to the meat, then strain in the coconut liquid, stirring all the time. Season with salt. Cover and cook in a slow oven, 150 °C/300 °F., Gas Mark 1–2, for 3 hours. Taste and adjust the seasoning before serving, with the rice and poppadums.

Danish Plum Layer

650 g/1½ lb. plums
100 g/4 oz. soft brown sugar
2 tablespoons water
50 g/2 oz. butter
100 g/5 oz. wholemeal breadcrumbs
1.5 dl/¼ pint double cream
15 g/1½ oz. chocolate, grated

Stone the plums and put into a saucepan with three-quarters of the sugar and the water. Cover the pan and simmer gently for 10 minutes or until the plums are quite tender. Remove from the heat, purée until smooth, then turn into the bottom of a glass serving dish and allow to cool. Melt the butter in a frying pan and fry the breadcrumbs until they are quite crisp. Remove from the heat, stir in the remaining sugar and allow to cool, then sprinkle over the top of the plums. Whip the cream until it just holds its shape and spread carefully over the top of the crumbs, then sprinkle over the grated chocolate. Chill until ready to serve.

Portuguese
Supper

for Winter or Autumn

MENU

Fresh Sardines with Tomatoes
Sauté Potatoes
Courgettes
Orange Crème Caramel

[Serves 4]

Nothing, of course, complements Mateus Rosé better than Portuguese food, and Portugal is particularly well known for its excellent fish, especially shellfish. Much of the shellfish is not readily available here, and crayfish, lobsters, etc. are prohibitively expensive; however fresh sardines, once a rare sight, can now be found in many fishmongers and can also be bought frozen.

The Portuguese also excel themselves at making any number of different crème caramels which they call 'Pudim' or 'Pudim flan'. This particular crème must be served very cold as it is quite sweet, so some readers may like to reduce the quantity of sugar by 25 g/1 oz.

Fresh Sardines with Tomatoes

3 tablespoons olive oil
1 Spanish onion, peeled and chopped
1 clove garlic, crushed
1.5 dl/¼ pint Mateus Rosé
450 g/1 lb. tomatoes, peeled and chopped
salt and freshly milled black pepper
650 g/1½ lb. fresh sardines
2 tablespoons fresh white breadcrumbs

Heat 2 tablespoons of the oil in a pan and gently fry the onion and garlic for 5 minutes. Add the wine and cook rapidly until the wine has been reduced by half. Add the tomatoes and seasoning, and cook gently for 20 minutes stirring from time to time. Taste and adjust the seasoning; then turn into an ovenproof dish. Clean the sardines, lay them on top of the tomato sauce and brush each one with a little olive oil. Season with salt and pepper and sprinkle over the breadcrumbs. Bake in a moderately hot oven, 200 °C/400 °F., Gas Mark 6, for 30 minutes until the breadcrumbs are crisp and golden brown.

Orange Crème Caramel

15 g/$\frac{1}{2}$ oz. butter
100 g/4 oz. granulated sugar
4 tablespoons water
juice 3 oranges
6 egg yolks

To decorate (optional)
peeled rind 1 orange

Lightly butter a 9 dl/$1\frac{1}{2}$ pint ovenproof dish. Put the sugar and water into a small, strong saucepan and put over a gentle heat until the sugar has dissolved. Increase the heat and boil rapidly until a pale golden caramel is reached. Pour half of this into the bottom of the prepared dish and leave to set. Add the orange juice to the remaining caramel in the pan and replace over a very gentle heat until the caramel has dissolved. Remove from the heat and allow to cool to blood heat. Beat the egg yolks then beat in the orange caramel mixture. Pour into the prepared dish. Cover with foil and stand in a roasting tin containing 2.5 cm/1 inch cold water. Bake in a very low oven, 150 °C/300 °F., Gas Mark 1–2, for about 1 hour or until set. Allow to cool in the dish, chill thoroughly then invert on to a clean serving plate. If liked the caramel can be decorated before serving as in the picture. Cut the thinly peeled orange rind into very fine shreds, then plunge into boiling water for 1 minute. Drain and dry thoroughly and pile on top of the caramel.

Work Plan

The day before or earlier in the day
★ **Make Orange Crème Caramel.**

In the afternoon
★ **Put Mateus Rosé into fridge to chill.**
★ **Par-boil potatoes.**
★ **Prepare courgettes.**

Before serving
★ **Prepare tomato sauce 1$\frac{1}{4}$ hours before serving.**
★ **Put sardines into oven 30 minutes before serving.**
★ **Cook potatoes and courgettes just before serving.**

PART THREE
DINNER PARTIES

*G*ood food, good wine and good company are the three important ingredients for a successful dinner party; whilst I cannot guarantee the last, if you follow these menus you will certainly be able to fulfil the first two essentials. Dinner party food should not only taste superb, but should be elegant as well, with the different courses complementing each other in flavour, colour and texture.

All the menus have a cold starter and dessert, which can be prepared well in advance, leaving you with plenty of time to concentrate on the main course and vegetables. Correct cooking of vegetables is very important as they really can make or mar a meal; in fact I usually judge restaurants by the way they have cooked and serve the vegetables, as it often tells you more about their cooking than the main dish does.

Although you can of course use frozen vegetables, as I have suggested in the dinners for two, and they certainly have their place in modern living, for dinner parties I prefer to serve fresh, seasonal vegetables. Most British people like potatoes with their meal, although for the Spring Menu I have suggested serving freshly boiled noodles as, certainly in early spring, old potatoes are past their prime, whilst there is usually a scarcity of good new potatoes at a realistic price. In summer, though, there is little to beat the flavour of new potatoes, either lightly scraped or cooked in their skins, boiled or steamed with a sprig of mint, then drained and tossed with melted butter and chopped parsley, chives or chervil. For autumn I have suggested serving Stovie Potatoes; layered potatoes and onions, casseroled slowly in the oven in milk, or mixed milk and cream for a richer dish, whilst for winter, Jacket Potatoes make a perfect accompaniment to a Game Casserole, served either with butter or a spoonful of soured cream.

Green vegetables are nicest if they are served as soon as they are cooked, although you can keep them warm for about 10–15 minutes after cooking if necessary. When cooking carrots by the conservative method suggested on page 31, you can also add a teaspoon of sugar to the cooking liquor which will lightly glaze them, or add a few herbs to the cooking liquor for added flavour. On page 38 I have suggested ways in which you can jazz-up Brussels sprouts for the Winter Menu if you do not want to serve them plain, as well as giving instructions in the relevant menus for cooking spinach and French beans to retain the maximum food value and flavour. Always remember that vegetables should not be over-cooked, as this destroys, not only their taste and texture, but their nutritional value as well.

As well as the food for the dinner party, you may also like to serve a few savoury tit-bits with drinks before the meal, although I am not very keen on giving people *too* much to eat at this stage of the evening, or they can lose their appetite — very disheartening when you have spent hours slaving over the cooker. One of the nicest savoury biscuits I have ever tasted was given to me recently by a friend who then kindly parted with the recipe. The great bonus about Sarah's cheese biscuits is that not only do they taste delicious, but you can keep the unbaked dough made up in the fridge for a week or two, wrapped in greasproof paper and use it when you want, or you can deep freeze it. You need equal quantities of plain flour, butter and finely grated Cheddar cheese (100 g/4 oz. each will make about 30 biscuits), and a pinch of salt, black pepper and cayenne. Rub the butter into the flour and seasonings, then add the cheese and mix to a dough with your hands. Knead on a lightly floured surface, form into a long roll 4 cm/1½ inches in diameter, wrap in greaseproof paper and put into the fridge. When ready to bake, cut into slices, about 0.5 cm/scant ¼ inch thick. Place on greased baking trays, brush with a little beaten egg and bake in a moderately hot oven, 190 °C/375 °F., Gas Mark 5, for about 10 minutes or until golden brown.

If you feel you have the time, the flavour of home-salted nuts is very much better than that of bought ones. Fry blanched almonds, peanuts, cashew nuts or hazel-nuts in a little oil until golden brown. Remove from the pan, drain on kitchen paper, then sprinkle with salt, preferably sea salt. Another of my favourites is lightly toasted sunflower seeds. Cover the rack of the grill pan with foil, sprinkle over shucked sunflower seeds and toast under a low grill until they are golden brown.

Spring Dinner Party

MENU

Avocado and Salami Salad

Pork Escalopes with Fennel
and Cream Sauce

Freshly Boiled Noodles

Carrots

Grape Meringue Shortcake

[Serves 6]

Spring is always thought of as a 'green' time of the year, when all the new leaves and shoots suddenly appear that beautiful pale green colour which only lasts for a few weeks to be replaced with the deeper green of summer. The Avocado and Salami Salad has just that pale green colour about it, interspersed with pieces of rich red salami and pepper.

The Pork Escalopes with Fennel are also a pale green, and then to give a little added colour there is the orange of the fresh, young carrots. Many shops now sell pork escalopes, rather than veal, as it is so much more easily obtainable and they make an excellent elegant dinner party dish. The pleasant aniseed tang of the fennel marries well with the pork to give a slightly unusual sauce that is not difficult to make. Although the dish should be served as soon as possible after it has been

made, it can be kept hot, covered, for about 15 minutes or while you eat the first course.

Freshly boiled noodles are quick to prepare, although they really are at their best if you cook them just before serving and allow 150 g/6 oz. dry weight for six people. Fresh young carrots look attractive served whole, but if you have to use older carrots, cut them into sticks, or obliquely into slices to make them look more interesting and allow 900 g/2 lb. Always cook carrots slowly in the very minimum salted water and add a knob of butter to them as well, together with some herbs, if wished.

The Grape Meringue Shortcake goes away from the green theme, although you could use green grapes if you preferred. This is a practical recipe as the egg yolks are used in the shortcake, and the whites in the meringue, and these two have a pleasant contrasting texture.

Avocado and Salami Salad

3 ripe avocado pears
2 dl/generous ¼ pint mayonnaise
3 sticks celery, chopped
1 red pepper, de-seeded and finely chopped
50 g/2 oz. salami, cut into matchsticks
salt and freshly milled black pepper
a few drops Tabasco
few lettuce leaves

Cut the avocados in half and remove the stones. Scoop out the flesh with a teaspoon and toss quickly in the mayonnaise to preserve the colour. Add the celery and half the pepper and salami, then season to taste with salt, pepper and Tabasco. Pile back into the half avocado skins, arrange on individual plates with the lettuce leaves and cover until ready to serve, then remove covers and sprinkle with the remainder of the chopped pepper and salami before serving.

Work Plan

Earlier in the day

★ Put Mateus Rosé into fridge to chill.
★ Cook Grape Meringue Shortcake but do not fill.

Two hours before serving

★ Prepare Avocado and Salami salads.
★ Prepare all ingredients for pork.
★ Prepare the carrots and leave in cold water.
★ Complete the Grape Meringue Shortcake.

Before serving

★ Start to cook pork 20 minutes before serving.
★ Cook carrots and noodles just before serving.

Pork Escalopes with Fennel and Cream Sauce

1 large or two small heads fennel
100 g/4 oz. butter
2 shallots or small onions, peeled and finely chopped
1 tablespooon flour
salt and freshly milled black pepper
6 pork escalopes, each about 100 g/4 oz.
5 tablespoons Mateus Rosé
3 dl/½ pint single cream

Cut the fennel into fine slivers, discarding any very tough outer pieces and reserving any green fronds. Melt half the butter in a small pan and gently fry the fennel and onions for 10 minutes. Season the flour with salt and pepper and lightly toss each escalope in the seasoned flour. Melt the remaining butter in a large frying pan and fry the escalopes quickly on each side for about 3 minutes, without allowing the butter to burn. When the escalopes are tender, remove from the pan, place on a heated serving dish and keep warm. Add the cooked fennel and shallot or onion to the pan, then pour over the wine and boil rapidly for 2–3 minutes. Remove from the heat and stir in the cream and seasoning. Return to a very gentle heat and heat until piping hot, without allowing the sauce to boil. Pour over the escalopes and garnish with the green fennel fronds before serving.

Grape Meringue Shortcake

275 g/10 oz. plain flour
pinch of salt
125 g/5 oz. butter
175 g/7 oz. caster sugar
2 eggs, separated
1 tablespoon flaked almonds
1.5 dl/¼ pint double cream, whipped
350 g/12 oz. black grapes

Sift together the flour and salt. Rub in the butter until the mixture resembles fine breadcrumbs, then add 75 g/3 oz. of the sugar. Blend the egg yolks together. Add to the flour and mix to a stiff dough. Knead lightly on a floured working surface until smooth. Roll out on a greased baking tray to a 22.5 cm/9 inch circle. Prick with a fork and bake in a moderately hot oven, 190 °C/375 °F., Gas Mark 5, for 20 minutes. Reduce the oven temperature to 140 °C/275 °F., Gas Mark 1.

Whisk the egg whites until they form stiff peaks. Whisk in the remaining sugar a teaspoon at a time. Spoon tablespoons of the meringue round the edges of the shortcake or pipe using a rose nozzle. Sprinkle with the almonds and return to the cool oven for 30 minutes or until the meringue is crisp. Leave to cool on the baking tray for 10 minutes, then remove and cool on a wire rack.

Halve the grapes and remove the pips. Fold two-thirds of the grapes into the cream and pile into the centre of the cake. Decorate the top of the cream with the remainder of the grapes.

Summer Dinner Party

MENU

Devilled Crab Cocktail
Rack of Lamb en Croûte
Buttered New Potatoes
French Beans
Mateus Peaches

[Serves 6]

A light summer dinner party menu which looks impressive, but does not require too much elaborate preparation to make it so. A crab cocktail looks attractive and make a pleasant change from the more usual prawn and seafood cocktails and fresh crabs are generally fairly easily available during the summer months. However, should you have difficulty obtaining one, you could use 225 g/8 oz. canned or frozen crab meat instead.

The Rack of Lamb en Croûte may sound rather complicated, but in reality is not that difficult. You can use either English or New Zealand lamb for this, but it should not be too fatty. As a best end of neck of lamb only consists of eight chops, you will have to buy one of eight and one of four chops or two of six and join them together.

Whether you serve the new potatoes scraped, or simply wash them thoroughly and cook them in their skins is a matter of personal choice. Allow 900 g/2 lb. and always remember that the flavour is improved if a sprig of mint is added to the cooking water. As soon as they are cooked, drain them thoroughly, top them with butter and sprinkle them with a little chopped parsley or chopped chives. If the French beans are young they will only require topping and tailing, but if they are slightly older, the sides may need stringing as well. They should be plunged into rapidly boiling salted water and cooked until they are just tender, then drained; allow 450–550 g/1–1¼ lb. as there is little wastage.

The Mateus peaches require almost no preparation, and can be prepared several hours in advance, although they should not be made the day before or the peaches will become slightly soggy and have a tendency to discolour. It is most important however, that they are served well chilled and they make a very simple, but refreshing dessert.

Devilled Crab Cocktail

1 crab, weighing approx. 650 g/1½ lb.
1.5 dl/¼ pint mayonnaise
1.5 dl/¼ pint soured cream
1 tablespoon tomato ketchup
½–1 teaspoon made mustard
2 sticks celery, finely chopped
a few drops Tabasco
salt and freshly milled black pepper
1 large lettuce heart

To garnish
paprika

To dress the crab, first ask the fishmonger to open the crab for you; if you are worried about which are the inedible parts he will usually show you, but they are not difficult to find. Pull the body away from the shell and discard the greyish-white stomach sac, and all the white tentacles which are also known as ladies fingers; once this is done, the remainder of the crab is edible. Remove all the brown meat from the shell and, if you have a female crab, remove the coral and put on one side. Pull off the legs and the claws from the body, and crack open the two large claws with a rolling pin, hammer or meat mallet and remove all the meat. Crack and take the meat out of two of the legs; break off the first joint of each of the six remaining legs, crack and remove the meat. Put the lower parts of the legs into the fridge and reserve for garnishing the cocktail. Cut the body in half and using a skewer, carefully remove all the meat from the leg sockets. Mix all the crab meat with the mayonnaise, soured cream, tomato ketchup, mustard, celery and green pepper. Season to taste with salt, pepper and a few drops of Tabasco. Put into a bowl, cover and refrigerate until required. Thirty minutes before serving, cut the lettuce heart into quarters, wash and dry thoroughly. Shred the lettuce and divide between 6 glasses. Spoon the crab mixture on top and garnish each glass with a crab claw, and the reserved roe lightly sprinkled on the top, or a little paprika.

Rack of Lamb en Croûte

2 best ends of neck of lamb consisting of a total of
12 cutlets
salt and freshly milled black pepper
1 tablespoon oil
1 medium-sized onion, peeled and finely chopped
100 g/4 oz. mushrooms, finely chopped
2 tablespoons chopped parsley
a good pinch dried rosemary
370 g/13½ oz. packet frozen puff pastry, de-frosted
beaten egg for glazing

Make a cut all the way along the top of the joints of meat about 5 cm/2 inches from the end of the bones. Cut away the meat to expose the ends of the cutlet bones and scrape off all the meat. Remove the skin if the butcher has not already done so and cut away some of the excess fat. Join the two best ends together by sewing with two or three stitches using coarse thread or fine string. Season the meat with salt and pepper.

Heat the oil in a large frying pan, and fry the meat on all sides so that it is well sealed. Remove from the pan and put on one side. Pour off all but 1 tablespoon fat from the pan. Finely chop any lean meat that has been removed from the bones and add to the pan with the onion. Fry gently for 5 minutes, then add the mushrooms and cook gently for a further 5 minutes. Add the herbs and season to taste. Roll out the pastry until it is large enough to envelop the meat completely, leaving the scraped bones exposed. Trim the edges and brush the edges with beaten egg. Spread the stuffing carefully in a line over one-third of the top of the pastry. Lay the meat on top with the fat side to the stuffing. Bring up the bottom half of the pastry and seal all the edges well. Place on a greased baking sheet with the rounded side uppermost. Roll out the pastry trimmings and cut into leaves and flowers to decorate the top. Brush with egg and place in position. Cover and put into the fridge until ready to bake.

Before baking, brush all over with beaten egg and cook in a moderately hot oven 200 °C/400 °F., Gas Mark 6, for 1 hour. Brush the pastry once more with egg during cooking; if the pastry is getting a little too brown, cover with a sheet of greaseproof paper. Remove from the oven, place on a heated serving dish, and top each bone with a cutlet frill.

Mateus Peaches

½ bottle Mateus Rosé
6 large peaches
3 tablespoons caster sugar

Thoroughly chill the Mateus Rosé in the fridge. Peel the peaches; if they are difficult to peel, plunge them into boiling water for 1 minute, then drain and peel. Slice the peaches, remove the stones and place in one large or individual serving dishes. Sprinkle over the sugar, then pour over the Mateus Rosé and stir gently. Cover and chill in the fridge until required.

Autumn
Dinner Party

MENU

Aubergine Pâté
Braised Beef with Soured Cream
Stovie Potatoes
Leaf Spinach
Pears with Chocolate Mousse

[Serves 6]

This is a very simple menu for the hostess to prepare and serve, as it requires very little last-minute preparation apart from cooking the spinach, and makes the best possible use of autumn produce. It is said that there are literally hundreds of different ways of cooking aubergines in the Middle East and there are certainly countless variations of this aubergine pâté, which is also known as Poor Man's Caviar because of its blackish-grey colour. It is best served with warm pitta which you can just heat in the oven with the beef for 5 minutes before serving, but the pâté itself can be made much earlier in the day or even the day before as the flavour improves if it is left for several hours before serving.

In the Braised Beef with Soured Cream the meat is kept in large pieces, rather than cut into cubes, which makes a rather more elegant dinner party dish. Skirt beef is one of the best stewing cuts as it becomes very tender with long, slow cooking and the marbling of a small amount of fat with the lean helps to keep it moist, whilst there is no excess fat round it. However, it is not always possible to buy, as there is only a small amount on any one animal, so good-quality chuck steak could be used instead.

The Stovie Potatoes cook in the oven at the same time as the meat, although they must be put in the oven earlier to ensure that they are really well cooked. The grated cheese on top makes it an attractive golden brown, as well as adding to the flavour. Spinach, of course, goes down a great deal on cooking owing to its high water content, so you need to allow 1.25 kg/3 lb. It is best when cooked purely in its own water; wash the spinach in several changes of cold water to make sure you have removed all the grit. Melt 25 g/1 oz. butter in a large pan, then add the spinach, season with salt, cover the pan and simmer gently for about 10 minutes or until the spinach is quite tender. Drain and serve.

Almost everyone likes chocolate mousse, especially the men, but it can be very rich and the stuffed pears served with it here make a very pleasant contrast. If you wish to place the pears on top of the mousse, as in the photograph, you will not be able to complete the dessert until about 1 hour before serving as, even with lemon brushed over them, the pears tend to discolour. However, you can put the pears into the serving dish first (brush them with a little lemon juice), then pour the chocolate mousse over them and decorate the top when the mousse has set; the dessert can then be prepared the day before if wished.

Aubergine Pâté

2–3 aubergines (about 650 g/1½ lb.)
6 anchovy fillets
6 tablespoons olive oil
juice 1 lemon
1–2 cloves garlic, crushed
salt and freshly milled black pepper

To garnish
onion rings

Lightly score the aubergine skins. Put the aubergines on a baking tray and bake in a moderate oven, 180 °C/ 350 °F., Gas Mark 4, for 1 hour or until they are completely soft. When cool enough to handle, cut in half and scoop out the pulp. Put into a blender with the anchovy fillets and blend until smooth, or put into a bowl and pound until smooth. Gradually beat in the oil, then the lemon juice, garlic and seasoning. Put into a serving dish and garnish with onion rings. Serve with hot pitta.

Braised Beef with Soured Cream

6 pieces skirt beef or good-quality braising steak,
each about 225 g/8 oz.
25 g/1 oz. butter
2 tablespoons oil
225 g/8 oz. button onions, peeled
1½ tablespoons paprika
40 g/1½ oz. flour
4.5 dl/¾ pint beef stock
2 tablespoons tomato purée
salt and freshly milled black pepper
1 sprig fresh thyme or ½ teaspoon dried thyme
2 dill cucumbers, chopped
2 teaspoons capers
1.5 dl/¼ pint soured cream

Trim the meat and cut off any excess fat. Heat the butter and oil in a fireproof casserole, and quickly fry the pieces of meat, two at a time, until browned on all sides. Remove from the pan and put on one side. Add the onions to the fat remaining in the pan and fry gently for 5 minutes. Stir in the paprika and flour and cook, stirring frequently, for 2 minutes. Gradually stir in the stock and tomato purée and bring to the boil, stirring all the time. Season with salt and pepper and add the thyme, dill cucumbers and capers. Replace the meat in the casserole, cover and cook in a very moderate oven, 170 °C/325 °F., Gas Mark 3, for 2 hours. Arrange the pieces of beef on a heated serving dish, stir the cream into the hot sauce, and heat gently without allowing the sauce to boil. Taste and adjust the seasoning, then pour the sauce over the meat and serve as soon as possible.

Stovie Potatoes

Peel and slice 1.25 kg/3 lb. potatoes and 450 g/1 lb. onions. Put the potatoes and onions into a well-buttered ovenproof dish in layers, seasoning each layer with salt, freshly milled black pepper and a little grated nutmeg. Pour over 3 dl/½ pint milk or mixed milk and single cream, dot the top of the potatoes with 25 g/1 oz. butter and cover tightly. Bake in a very moderate oven, 170 °C/325 °F., Gas Mark 3, for 2 hours. Remove the lid, sprinkle the top with 50 g/2 oz. grated cheese, then return to the oven for a further 45 minutes until the top is golden brown.

Work Plan

Earlier in the day or the day before
★ Make Aubergine Pâté and keep in fridge until 1 hour before serving.
★ Make Pears with Chocolate Mousse (see note above) and keep in fridge until ready to serve.

In the afternoon
★ Put Mateus Rosé into fridge to chill.

In the late afternoon
★ Prepare potatoes and put in oven.
★ Prepare beef and put in oven.
★ Wash spinach and leave in cold water.

Before serving
★ Sprinkle cheese over potatoes 45 minutes before serving.
★ Complete Pears with Chocolate Mousse (see note above).
★ Cook spinach just before serving.
★ Heat pitta for 5 minutes before serving.

Pears with Chocolate Mousse

125 g/5 oz. plain chocolate
1 tablespoon strong black coffee
4 eggs, separated
3 large ripe pears
a little lemon juice
2 tablespoons finely chopped hazelnuts
1 tablespoon finely chopped glacé cherries
1 tablespoon finely chopped candied peel

To decorate
1.5 dl/¼ pint double cream
a few glacé cherries and whole hazelnuts

Break the chocolate into small pieces, put into a basin with the coffee and stand over a pan of hot water until the chocolate has melted. Remove from the heat and beat in the egg yolks, one at a time. Whisk the egg whites until they form stiff peaks, then fold into the chocolate mixture. Pour into a serving dish and leave to set. Peel the pears, cut them in half and scoop out the cores, then brush all over with a little lemon juice to preserve the colour. Mix the nuts, cherries and candied peel together and divide this mixture between the pears, stuffing it well into the hole where the cores were removed. Place the pears, rounded side up on top of the chocolate mousse. Whip the cream until stiff, then pipe over the top of the pears and chocolate and decorate with the cherries and hazelnuts.

Variations: If wished, you can also add 2 tablespoons rum or brandy or the grated rind and juice of a small sweet orange. Combine the rum, brandy or juice with egg yolks and proceed as above.

Winter Dinner Party

MENU

Swan Downer
Game Casserole
Baked Jacket Potatoes
Brussels Sprouts
Ice Cream Bombe

[Serves 6]

Now that one can buy most fruit and vegetables throughout the year, planning interesting winter meals is much easier than it used to be, although I still prefer serving fresh, seasonal vegetables whenever possible. Blackcurrants, however, freeze very well and, as their summer season is comparatively short, they make a pleasant re-appearance as what is perhaps a rather unseasonal dessert, but one that finishes off this meal extremely well.

The Swan Downer is a delicious, but rather unusual starter, consisting of prawns in cream with garlic and herbs, very lightly set with a little aspic. It looks very attractive in small ramekins and is then easy to eat with a teaspoon, although you could make it in a larger dish if you preferred.

For the game casserole you can use any game you choose, either fresh or frozen. It is best made the day before as suggested in the recipe; the flavour is improved if it is left for a day, and you are then able to easily remove all the fat which comes to the surface of the cooking liquor, although the amount present will vary according to the game used. Cooking it the day before also ensures that the birds are quite tender as older game birds can take up to 4 hours to be really tender and, having once suffered the embarrassment of having to keep guests waiting for over an hour while a particularly tough grouse cooked, I know how awkward it can be.

The Baked Jacket Potatoes will need about 1½ hours if they are cooked in a very moderate oven when the casserole is reheated, and up to 2 hours if they are very large. Remember to prick them with a fork before placing in the oven, and if you like a crisp skin to them, brush the skins with a little oil as well. They can either be served with butter or a spoonful of soured cream, as in the photograph. The Brussels sprouts will just need to

be boiled or steamed for about 10 minutes according to size, but should be cooked just before serving. Allow 900 g/2 lb. To add a little interest to the sprouts you could add 25 g/1 oz. split blanched almonds fried in 25 g/1 oz. butter until browned or, if you preferred, sprinkle them with crisply fried breadcrumbs before serving.

The Ice Cream Bombe makes a very impressive dessert without being too rich, consisting of vanilla ice cream on the outside and blackcurrant sorbet on the inside. Most ice creams and sorbets are best not served straight from the freezer, so if you remove this from the freezer and put it in the fridge when you serve the main course it should be at just the right temperature when you are ready to serve it.

Swan Downer

3 dl/½ pint packet aspic jelly
1.5 dl/¼ pint double cream
1.5 dl/¼ pint single cream
225 g/8 oz. peeled prawns
1 clove garlic, crushed
2 tablespoons chopped parsley
a pinch dried tarragon
a pinch dried dill
salt and freshly milled black pepper

To garnish (optional)
6 whole prawns

Make up the aspic jelly according to the instructions on the packet and allow to cool. Whip the double and single cream together until as stiff as possible, then add the prawns, reserving about 18 for garnishing, together with any liquid if using frozen prawns, the garlic, parsley, tarragon and dill. Fold gently into the cream and, when the aspic is beginning to stiffen slightly but not set, fold half of this into the prawn mixture. Taste and adjust the seasoning and put in the fridge until almost thickened, then stir gently, spoon into 6 small ramekins and leave to set. If the reserved aspic has set, put into a small saucepan over a low heat, or stand the

container over a pan of hot water and leave until it has melted. Spoon a very thin layer of this over each prawn cream, then arrange the reserved prawns attractively on the top. Spoon over the remaining aspic and chill until ready to serve. Serve with brown bread and butter and garnish with whole prawns if wished.

Game Casserole

2 pheasants, 6 partridge, quail or pigeons,
or 3 wild duck
225 g/8 oz. fairly lean bacon, cut in one piece
2 tablespoons oil
3 onions, peeled and finely chopped
4 sticks celery, finely chopped
6 dl/1 pint stock
3 dl/$\frac{1}{2}$ pint Mateus Rosé
1 small bay leaf
1 sprig parsley
1 sprig thyme
6 juniper berries, crushed
rind $\frac{1}{2}$ orange
salt and freshly milled black pepper
little lard or bacon dripping (optional)
50 g/2 oz. flour
100 g/4 oz. mushrooms

Cut the birds into joints if large, or leave partridge, quail or pigeons whole. Cut the bacon into 1.5 cm/$\frac{1}{2}$ inch dice, discarding all the skin. Heat the oil in a large frying pan and gently fry the bacon for 10 minutes, remove from the pan with a draining spoon and put into a casserole. Add the game to the pan and fry quickly until browned on all sides, then remove from the pan with a draining spoon and place in the casserole. Add the onions and celery to the fat remaining in the pan and fry gently for 8 minutes. Add the stock and Mateus Rosé and stir well, then pour over the meat in the casserole. Add the herbs, orange rind and juniper berries and season with salt and pepper. Cover the casserole and cook in a very moderate oven, 170 °C/325 °F., Gas Mark 3, for 2–4 hours or until tender.

Work Plan

The day before
★ Prepare Game Casserole.
★ Make Ice Cream Bombe.

In the afternoon
★ Put Mateus Rosé into fridge to chill.
★ Decorate Ice Cream Bombe.
★ Complete Game Casserole.
★ Prepare vegetables.
★ Make Swan Downers and keep in fridge until ready to serve.

Before serving
★ Put potatoes into oven 1$\frac{1}{2}$ hours before serving.
★ Put Game Casserole into oven 45 minutes before serving.
★ Cook Brussels sprouts just before serving.

Remove from the oven, allow to cool, then put into the fridge overnight. The following day, skim off all the fat from the top of the casserole; weigh this and make up to 50 g/2 oz. with a little lard or bacon dripping, if necessary. Remove the herbs and orange rind. Melt the lard or dripping in a saucepan, stir in the flour and cook over a very gentle heat for about 10 minutes, stirring frequently until the flour is a rich brown colour; it must not be allowed to burn. Gradually stir in the cooking liquor from the casserole and bring to the boil, stirring all the time. Add all the remaining contents of the casserole, stir well, then return to the casserole. Add the mushrooms and reheat when required in a very moderate oven for 45 minutes before serving. Taste and adjust the seasoning before serving.

Ice Cream Bombe

For the ice cream
2 eggs, separated
50 g/2 oz. sifted icing sugar
¼ teaspoon vanilla essence
1.5 dl/¼ pint double cream, lightly whipped

For the blackcurrant sorbet
225 g/8 oz. frozen blackcurrants
100 g/4 oz. granulated sugar
1.5 dl/¼ pint water plus 4 tablespoons
1 egg white

To decorate
1.5 dl/¼ pint double cream, lightly whipped

Take two pudding basins, one 1.8 litres/3 pints and the other 6 dl/1 pint in capacity. Put the egg yolks into a basin with half the sugar and the vanilla essence and whisk until the mixture is thick and creamy. Whisk the egg whites in a separate basin and gradually whisk in the remaining sugar, a teaspoon at a time. Continue whisking and gradually beat in the whisked egg yolks. Stop beating and then fold in the whipped cream. Turn this ice cream mixture into the larger pudding basin, then carefully drop the smaller basin into the centre so that when the ice cream freezes there will be a hole in the centre. Freeze the ice cream until firm.

Put the blackcurrants into a saucepan with the 4 tablespoons water. Cover and cook gently for 10 minutes or until the blackcurrants are quite tender. Remove from the heat and purée, either in a blender or by rubbing through a fine sieve. Put the granulated sugar and remaining water into a small pan, heat gently until the sugar has melted, then boil rapidly for 5 minutes. Remove from the heat and stir into the blackcurrant purée. Turn into a small container and freeze until the mixture is half-frozen.

Remove the ice cream from the freezer and pour a little hot water into the small basin. Leave for a couple of minutes (this will melt the ice cream round the edge of the basin so that it is easy to remove); then replace in the freezer for 5 minutes so that the ice cream can harden again. Remove the blackcurrant mixture from the freezer and beat thoroughly with an electric mixer or whisk. Whisk the egg white until stiff, then carefully fold into the blackcurrant mixture. Pour the black-currant sorbet into the centre hole of the ice cream, cover and freeze the mixture until required. To turn the ice cream out, simply dip the bowl into a little hot water to just melt the ice cream round the edge, then invert on to a serving dish, clean up the edges, and put back into the freezer for 10 minutes to allow the ice cream to harden again. Using a piping bag and 1.5 cm/½ inch rose nozzle, pipe cream round the sides and top of the bombe to decorate it, then replace in the freezer. Remove the bombe from the freezer 30 minutes before serving and put into the fridge to soften slightly.

Dinner for Two

MENU

*Dublin Bay Prawns with
Devilled Mayonnaise
Roast Duckling with
Grape and Orange Sauce
Game Chips
Buttered Frozen Peas
Mateus Syllabub*

Dinner for two for a special occasion demands rather special food, although you may not necessarily have too much time to prepare it. This is a non-seasonal meal which you could easily prepare in the evening after you have got back from work, or put the children to bed, although try to remember to put the Mateus Rosé into the fridge earlier in the day.

The prawns need no preparation and are served simply with a piquant mayonnaise. The duckling is plainly roasted and served with potato crisps, which can be heated in the oven for 5 minutes, and frozen peas. The syllabub can be made quickly with an electric mixer, but do start whisking slowly or you will spatter the whole kitchen with syllabub.

Dublin Bay Prawns with Devilled Mayonnaise

8 large Dublin Bay prawns, or
225 g/8 oz. prawns in their shells
a few lettuce leaves
lemon wedges
4 tablespoons mayonnaise
a few drops Tabasco
4 spring onions, finely chopped
4 stuffed olives, finely chopped
1 tablespoon chopped parsley
salt and freshly milled black pepper

Arrange the prawns on two small plates and garnish with the lettuce leaves and lemon wedges. Put the mayonnaise into a basin and add the Tabasco, spring onions, olives and parsley. Season to taste and serve this sauce with the prawns.

Work Plan

Earlier in the day
★ Put Mateus Rosé into fridge to chill.

1½ hours before serving
★ Put duck into oven to roast
★ Prepare syllabub and put in fridge.
★ Place prawns on plates and prepare mayonnaise.

Before serving
★ Cook peas just before serving.
★ Make orange and grape sauce 5 minutes before serving.
★ Put crisps into oven 5 minutes before serving.

Duckling with Black Grape and Orange Sauce

1.8 kg/4 lb. duckling
salt and freshly milled black pepper
1 large orange
1 small onion, peeled and halved
100 g/4 oz. black grapes, halved and pipped
15 g/½ oz. sugar
3 teaspoons cornflour

Remove any giblets which may be inside the duck. Peel off the rind from half the orange and put inside the duck with the onion. Place in a roasting tin and prick all over the duck skin with a fork, then season with salt and pepper. Roast in a moderately hot oven, 200 °C/400 °F., Gas Mark 6, for 1¼–1½ hours until the skin of the duck is crisp and golden brown. Grate the remainder of the orange rind and squeeze all the juice. Pour the juice into a measuring jug and make up to 3 dl/½ pint with water. Pour all but 2 tablespoons into a small pan, add the sugar and heat gently until the sugar has dissolved, then bring to the boil. Blend the remainder of the orange juice with the cornflour in a small basin. Pour over the boiling orange mixture, stirring all the time, then return to the saucepan and bring back to the boil, stirring continuously. Add the grapes to the sauce and simmer gently for 2–3 minutes.

Mateus Syllabub

grated rind and juice ½ lemon
1 tablespoon caster sugar
5 tablespoons Mateus Rosé
1 dl/scant ¼ pint double cream

Whisk the cream, lemon rind and juice, caster sugar and half the Mateus Rosé in a bowl until the mixture holds its shape, then whisk in the remaining wine. Turn into two glasses and chill for at least 1 hour before serving.

Dinner for Two

from the Man's Point of View

MENU

Melon with Grapes
Lamb with Orange and Rosemary
Boiled Potatoes
Buttered Broad Beans
Italian Coffee Cream

Work Plan

Earlier in the day
★ Put Mateus Rosé into fridge to chill.

One hour before serving
★ Make Italian Coffee Cream and put in fridge until ready to serve.
★ Make Melon with Grapes and put in fridge until ready to serve.
★ Scrub potatoes and leave in cold water until ready to cook.

Before serving

★ Put potatoes on to cook 20 minutes before serving.
★ Start to cook lamb 20 minutes before serving.
★ Cook broad beans 10 minutes before serving or according to instructions on the packet.

Although there are a number of men who are superb cooks and really enjoy it, they are regrettably still in the minority. This very simple, but delicious, menu has been devised for those men who claim they are only capable of boiling eggs, but would occasionally like to give their ladies a treat!

Ogen or Charentais melons require no extra sugar to be added to them, but are enhanced by a little Mateus Rosé poured over them; the black grapes add some interesting colour, as well as flavour. They are best served chilled, but should not be chilled for too long, or the delicate flavour will be destroyed.

Although rosemary goes well with other meat and fish, it is traditionally used with lamb, but it has a very pungent smell and flavour, so you only need a very little to give the meat the flavour you require, without it becoming overpowering. Cooking potatoes in their skins is not only simpler, but this way you also retain the maximum food value as much of the vitamin content lies just under the skin of the potato. I have suggested serving frozen broad beans as a second vegetable, but you could of course use any other frozen or fresh vegetable you like. Allow 350 g/12 oz. potatoes and 225 g/8 oz. frozen shelled broad beans. The Italian Coffee Cream is a classic Italian recipe using cream cheese and coffee. It is extremely simple to make and, as it is very rich, you only need a little of it.

Melon with Grapes

1 Ogen or Charentais melon
about 10 black grapes
about 2 tablespoons Mateus Rosé

Cut the melon in half and scoop out the seeds. Halve the grapes, remove the pips and pile into the centre hole. Spoon over the Mateus Rosé and chill for at least 30 minutes, but no more than 1 ½ hours, before serving.

Lamb with Orange and Rosemary

1 tablespoon oil
15 g/½ oz. butter
2 chump chops or fillet slices from the leg
grated rind and juice ½ small orange
1 sprig fresh or a good pinch dried rosemary
salt and freshly milled black pepper

To garnish (optional)
few slices fresh orange
few sprigs rosemary

Heat the oil and butter in a frying pan and quickly fry the meat for 5 minutes on each side. Add the orange rind and juice, rosemary and seasoning. Cover the pan and simmer gently for 10 minutes. Taste and adjust the seasoning before serving, garnished with the orange slices and rosemary if wished.

Italian Coffee Cream

100 g/4 oz. cream cheese
2 tablespoons soured cream
1 tablespoon caster sugar
1 teaspoon instant coffee

To decorate
2 coffee beans

Beat all the ingredients together until smooth. Leave for 2–3 minutes for the coffee to dissolve completely, then beat again. Pack into small pots, top each one with a coffee bean and chill for at least 1 hour or until required.

Note: For a more extravagant version of this cream, add 2 tablespoons of a coffee liqueur such as Tia Maria or Kahlua and beat with all the other ingredients.
Chill and decorate as above.

PART FOUR
BUFFET PARTIES

Buffet Parties are the obvious way to entertain a large number of people. In this chapter I have given menus for a Summer Special Occasion Buffet which serves 24 and a more modest Winter Buffet for 12 people.

When catering on this scale it is not always possible to put everything one wants into the fridge, unless you have a particularly large one, so I have indicated in the Work Plans which dishes should be stored in the fridge and which can be kept covered in a cool place. You are also unlikely to have room in the fridge for the Mateus Rosé, so the best way to chill it is in a large bucket of ice. If you have a freezer you can build up a large stock of ice over several days just by filling up all your available ice trays. When they have frozen, tip the ice cubes into a large polythene bag, store it in the freezer, then freeze a fresh batch.

However, if you do not have a freezer, or your freezer is full to capacity, you can usually buy large bags of ice from your wine merchant or off-licence, so check this out several days in advance. Put half the ice into a large bucket, put in the bottles of Mateus Rosé, then pour over the remainder of the ice, so that the bottles are almost completely submerged in the ice; it will take about 1 hour for the wine to become thoroughly chilled.

If you do not have sufficient glasses most off-licences will also lend you glasses free of charge, provided you buy the wine from them and, if you are a little worried about how much wine to allow, will usually let you buy the wine on a sale or return basis so that you can take back any bottles you do not use.

For a buffet when all the food is laid out on the table, presentation is very important. Salads in particular can be made to look very attractive and it is well worthwhile spending a little extra time making them really look appetizing. All these salad recipes have been chosen with an eye to their appearance, as well as their taste; the green of the apple skin contrasting with the dark red of the beetroot; the mixture of colours in the Courgette and Tomato Salad; the red of the tomatoes with the black olives garnishing the Crushed Wheat Salad; the sprinkling of red paprika on the Cauliflower Cheese Salad; the contrasting colours and textures in the Mixed Winter Salad – all make for dishes which are as pleasant to look at as they are to eat.

Piping cream on desserts gives them a very professional finish and is not a difficult art to master. Personally I think it is much easier to do with a simple nylon or plastic piping bag and nozzle, rather than with some of the icing kits consisting of metal tubes and similar gadgets which I find more difficult to work. To give yourself a little confidence to start with you can practise using some well-mashed potato (instant potato would be ideal) and see the different patterns and designs you can make even with one nozzle. When you have finished using it, take the nozzle out of the bag and wash both separately. The bag can sometimes be difficult to dry thoroughly with a tea towel, so leave it hanging somewhere near the cooker until it is quite dry.

Glazing savoury food with aspic is another way to make it look really elegant; you can make your own aspic, but it is a great deal of bother and most of the packets of aspic jelly powders on the market have quite a good flavour, especially some of the Continental ones. Always follow the instructions on the packet when making up the aspic; to improve the flavour you can replace up to 4 tablespoons water in 6 dl/1 pint with 4 tablespoons Mateus Rosé. In the majority of cases it is best to use the aspic when it is quite cold but has not quite set; should it set up too quickly you can always melt it again by standing in a container over a pan of gently simmering water. When the jelly has melted, remove from the heat, allow to cool and then use as required.

Special Occasion Summer Buffet

MENU

Fresh Salmon Mousse
Turkey Galantine
Crushed Wheat Salad
Beetroot and Apple Salad
Courgette Salad
Curried Mushroom Salad
Strawberry Charlotte Malakoff
Raspberry and Hazlenut Torte

[Serves 24]

This is rather an elaborate lunch or dinner for a special occasion, such as a wedding, christening, anniversary or even a birthday, and although none of the dishes are impossibly difficult or complicated, some of them do require a little time and patience.

Fresh Salmon Mousse makes a popular and uncomplicated starter and it is not necessary to use Scotch salmon for this; Canadian salmon, which can be as much as half the price of Scotch, is more than adequate. I do not personally like savoury mousses to be very firmly set, so if you wanted to make this mousse in a mould you would have to add some gelatine to it (a 15 g/½ oz. envelope dissolved in 4 tablespoons water would be enough). I have suggested a very simple garnish of prawns or shrimps in their shells which looks very effective, but you could of course garnish it in any way you wished.

Now that you can buy frozen turkeys in most large supermarkets and deep freeze shops throughout the year, they have ceased to be a Christmas-only treat. Whereas you would have to make two chicken galantines to feed this number of people a 4.5 kg/10 lb. turkey, when stuffed with other meats will feed 24 comfortably; slice for slice this galantine, as well as having a superb flavour, is also very good value for money. There is no denying that making it is time-consuming, but once prepared there is nothing to do at the last minute and if you do not want to go to the bother of making the chaudfroid sauce and glazing it, you could perfectly well just slice it and arrange it on a

serving platter garnished with tomatoes, watercress or mustard and cress, or you could just give it a simple aspic glaze, which again does not take too much time.

If you have never boned out a bird before there are a few golden rules. First of all you must use a fairly small sharp knife, or you will have problems getting the meat off the bone. Secondly, look at the bird very carefully and, if you are not sure exactly where all the joints are, feel where they are with your hands and by moving the legs and wings. Do not hurry the process, start at the back bone, cutting away from you all the time, sever the joints between the carcass and the legs and wings and carefully scrape all the meat off the bones. Do not worry too much if you pierce the skin as you can always sew up any holes with fine string or thread. Once you

46

have taken out all the bones, just lay the carcass out flat on a board and stuff it as described in the recipe. The bones should then all be put into a large pan and boiled up to make stock; always remember that if you do not want to use the stock immediately it freezes well.

I have deliberately served some slightly unusual salads with the galantine to get away from the more mundane rice, potato and tomato salads, although you could serve a tossed green salad as well if you wished. The Crushed Wheat Salad is an Arabian recipe and you can buy crushed wheat, which is also known as burghul or kibble, in most health food shops; everyone I have served it to always asks for the recipe, which I think speaks for itself. Raw mushrooms also make an excellent salad, as do blanched courgettes which,

combined with tomatoes make a very attractive salad.

Fresh strawberry and raspberry desserts always go down well and these are two rather special recipes. The Strawberry Charlotte Malakoff has a very rich filling of whipped cream, fresh strawberries, ground almonds and Mateus Rosé. You can serve it just on its own, or it is excellent served with a strawberry sauce made from fresh sweetened strawberries, puréed in a blender. The Raspberry and Hazlenut Torte consists of raspberries and cream layered between slices of a light hazelnut sponge with the top of the torte decorated with fresh raspberries and cream.

The Work Plan on page 48 has been planned around lunchtime, if you wish to serve this meal at night you can obviously make a few adjustments to the timing.

┌─────────────────────────────────────┐

Work Plan

Two days before
* ★ Defrost turkey.
* ★ Put apricots to soak overnight.
* ★ Put ham to soak overnight.
* ★ Cook salmon for mousse, cool and put in fridge.

The day before
* ★ Prepare Turkey Galantine, roast and allow to cool. Store in a cool place.
* ★ Make Salmon Mousse and keep in fridge until just before serving.
* ★ Make Strawberry Charlotte Malakoff and put in fridge.
* ★ Make hazelnut base for Raspberry and Hazelnut Torte.
* ★ Make Crushed Wheat Salad, cover and put in a cool place.
* ★ Make Curried Mushroom Salad, cover and put in a cool place.
* ★ Cook courgettes for salad, cover and put in a cool place.
* ★ Make dressing for remaining salads.

In the morning
* ★ Put Mateus Rosé to chill in fridge or in a large bucket of ice (see page 45).
* ★ Glaze and decorate Turkey Galantine.
* ★ Decorate Strawberry Charlotte Malakoff and keep in fridge until just before serving.
* ★ Assemble Raspberry and Hazelnut Torte and keep in fridge until required.
* ★ Complete all the salads.

└─────────────────────────────────────┘

Fresh Salmon Mousse

900 g/2 lb. fresh salmon
1 onion, peeled and sliced
1 lemon, sliced
a few parsley stalks
salt and freshly milled black pepper
4 tablespoons Mateus Rosé
6 dl/1 pint packet aspic jelly powder
4.5 dl/$\frac{3}{4}$ pint mayonnaise
125 g/5 oz. can tomato purée
2 cloves garlic, crushed
1 teaspoon dried tarragon
1 teaspoon anchovy essence
2 tablespoons chopped parsley
a few drops Tabasco
3 dl/$\frac{1}{2}$ pint double cream, lightly whipped

To garnish
100 g/4 oz. whole prawns or shrimps in their shells

Take a piece of foil large enough to completely envelop the salmon. Lay half the onion and lemon slices and the parsley stalks in the centre and season. Place the salmon

on top. Season, cover with the remaining onion and lemon slices and pour over the Mateus Rosé. Bring up the edges of the foil to form a parcel, place in a roasting tin and bake in a moderate oven. 180 °C/350 °F., Gas Mark 4, for 45 minutes. Remove from the oven and allow to cool in the foil. When the salmon is quite cold, discard the onion, parsley and lemon. Peel off the skin and mash the flesh together with all the cooking liquor, discarding all the bones. Make up the aspic jelly according to the instructions on the packet and allow to cool, but not set. Turn the salmon into a large mixing bowl and add the mayonnaise, tomato purée, garlic, tarragon, anchovy essence, parsley, Tabasco and seasoning. Fold half the cold aspic carefully into the salmon mixture, then fold in the whipped cream and taste and adjust the seasoning. Turn into a serving dish, place in the fridge and leave for 2 hours or until set.

If the remaining aspic sets, reheat gently in a basin over a pan of hot water until melted. Pour a very thin layer of gelatine over the surface of the mousse and allow to set. Arrange the prawns or shrimps attractively on the top, dipping them first in the liquid aspic, then pour over the last of the aspic and allow to set.

Turkey Galantine

4.5 kg/10 lb. oven-ready turkey
1.1 kg/2$\frac{1}{2}$ lb. joint lean hock
100 g/4 oz. dried apricots
the turkey heart and liver
900 g/2 lb. lean minced pork
2 tablespoons chopped parsley
grated rind 1 lemon
2 teaspoons dried marjoram
1 teaspoon dried thyme
1 teaspoon dried tarragon
salt and freshly milled black pepper
4 chicken breast joints
4 tablespoons Mateus Rosé
75 g/3 oz. butter
2 medium-sized onions, peeled and finely chopped

To garnish
6 dl/1 pint packet aspic jelly powder
4.5 dl/$\frac{3}{4}$ pint mayonnaise
tomatoes, lemons, cucumber skins,
pieces of tarragon, etc.

If the turkey is frozen allow to defrost overnight in the kitchen or for 24 hours in the fridge. Soak the bacon in a bowl of cold water for at least 6 hours or overnight; soak the apricots for 4 hours or overnight in cold water.

Place the turkey, breast side down, on a working surface. With a sharp knife cut through the back skin and flesh to the backbone, then carefully work the flesh away from the carcass, pressing the knife closely against the carcass and taking all the meat away from the bone with the skin. Split open the drumsticks to remove the bone, cut off the tips of the wings and discard. You will end up with a piece of meat with a large V in the centre as the legs are longer than the breast. Sew this up using a needle threaded with coarse thread or fine string, so that you end up with a large rectangle.

Finely mince the turkey liver and heart and add to the pork with the parsley, lemon rind, marjoram, thyme, tarragon and seasoning. Remove the meat from the chicken breasts (the skin and bones can be kept and used to make stock), cut the meat into strips about 1.5 cm/½ inch wide, season and put into the Mateus Rosé in a small dish. Leave to marinate for at least 30 minutes. Remove the bacon from the water, dry well, cut off the skin and then mince finely. Melt 25 g/1 oz. butter in a pan and gently fry the onions for 5 minutes, add to the minced bacon and season with plenty of black pepper. Drain the apricots.

Lay the turkey out flat with the skin underneath and season all over with salt and pepper. Spread half the pork mixture down the centre of the turkey, then lay half the strips of chicken on top, and cover with half the ham mixture. Lay the apricots in a line down the centre of the bird, then repeat the layers as before in reverse – ham, then chicken, then the last of the pork. Bring the edges of the skin together and form the mixture into a roll; using a needle with coarse thread or fine string, sew up so that all the stuffing is completely enclosed. Place in a roasting tin, spread all over with the remaining butter and season with salt and pepper. Cover with foil and roast in a moderate oven, 180 °C/350 °F., Gas Mark 4, for 4 hours, removing the cover for the last 30 minutes. Remove from the oven and allow to become quite cold.

Make up the aspic jelly according to the instructions on the packet and allow to cool, but not set, then carefully stir about half of it into the mayonnaise. Place the galantine on a wire rack with a tray underneath to catch all the drips. When the mayonnaise mixture is just beginning to stiffen, carefully pour all over the turkey. Leave this to set, then scoop up the drips from the tray, place in a basin over a pan of hot water and heat very gently until melted, then repeat this process once more. Use tomato skins, cucumber or tarragon and peeled lemon rind to make flowers, etc. Dip each piece of decoration in the remaining liquid aspic and place in position on the galantine. Allow to set, then pour the last of the aspic over the top and allow to set.

Crushed Wheat Salad

Put 350 g/12 oz. crushed wheat into a bowl and cover with cold water. Leave for 30 minutes during which time it will expand. Drain, then wrap in a tea towel and wring out to remove as much moisture as possible. Put into a bowl and add 2 finely chopped onions, 50 g/2 oz. finely chopped parsley, 50 g/2 oz. finely chopped mint, 6 tablespoons olive oil and 4 tablespoons lemon juice. Season to taste with salt and pepper. Pile into a serving dish and garnish with sliced tomatoes and black olives before serving.

Curried Mushroom Salad

Slice or quarter 650 g/1½ lb. button mushrooms, depending on size and turn into a bowl. Mix 3 dl/½ pint mayonnaise with 4 tablespoons French dressing, 2 tablespoons chutney and 1 tablespoon curry powder. Pour over the mushrooms, toss lightly together then pile into a serving dish. Garnish with paprika and watercress before serving.

Beetroot and Apple Salad

Peel 1.25 kg/3 lb. cooked beetroot and cut into 1.5 cm/½ inch dice. Add 2 green dessert apples, cored and diced and 4 sticks finely chopped celery, and toss together in 4 tablespoons French dressing. Pile into a serving dish and sprinkle with 2 tablespoons chopped chives before serving.

Courgette and Tomato Salad

Cut 900 g/2 lb. courgettes into thin slices. Blanch in boiling salted water for 1 minute, then dry thoroughly. Slice 900 g/2 lb. tomatoes, arrange both these and the courgettes in a serving dish, and season with salt and pepper. Add 1–2 cloves garlic to 6 tablespoons French dressing and mix well. Pour over the courgettes and tomatoes 1 hour before serving and sprinkle with chopped parsley.

Raspberry and Hazelnut Torte

225 g/8 oz. hazelnuts
8 eggs, separated
275 g/10 oz. caster sugar
450 g/1 lb. fresh raspberries
6 dl/1 pint double cream
extra caster sugar to sweeten raspberries

Grind the nuts in a blender or coffee mill. Grease a 30 × 35 cm/12 × 14 inch roasting tin, and line with greased greaseproof paper or silicone paper. Whisk the egg yolks and sugar until they are thick and creamy. Whisk the egg whites until they form stiff peaks, then fold the whisked egg whites and the nuts alternately into the egg yolks. Turn into the prepared tin, spread evenly and bake in a moderate oven, 180 °C/350 °F., Gas Mark 4, for 25–30 minutes or until set and golden brown. Allow to cool in the tin; if making the day before cover the whole roasting tin with foil to keep the cake moist.

Cut the cake into three strips, each 11 × 30 cm/ 4½ × 12 inches, and place one on a serving dish. Whip the cream until stiff, put about 4 tablespoons on one side for decorating and a few raspberries. Fold the remainder of the raspberries into the cream and sweeten to taste. Spread half the raspberry and cream mixture on the slice of cake on the dish, top with a second slice of cake, then the remaining raspberry mixture and finally the third slice of cake. Pipe the remaining cream on the top of the cake and decorate with the reserved raspberries.

Strawberry Charlotte Malakoff

225 g/8 oz. softened unsalted butter
150 g/6 oz. caster sugar
grated rind and juice 1 large orange
¼ teaspoon almond essence
3 dl/½ pint Mateus Rosé
150 g/6 oz. ground almonds
4.5 dl/¾ pint double cream
about 40 sponge finger (boudoir) biscuits
350 g/12 oz. fresh strawberries, sliced

To decorate
1.5 dl/¼ pint double cream, lightly whipped
100 g/4 oz. strawberries

Line the base of a loose-bottomed cake tin 20 cm/8 inches in diameter and 7.5 cm/3 inches deep with buttered greaseproof paper. Cream together the butter, sugar and orange rind until light and fluffy. Beat in the almond essence, then beat in 1.5 dl/¼ pint of the Mateus Rosé and the ground almonds alternately. Whip the double cream until it is just beginning to thicken, then fold into the almond mixture. Mix the remainder of the Mateus Rosé with the orange juice. Trim the sponge fingers so that they are the same length as the tin. Dip each sponge finger in the orange juice and Mateus mixture just for a second and use to line the sides of the prepared tin with the rounded end down. Dip the extra biscuits also in the wine mixture together with the trimmed ends and put on one side.

Spread a third of the almond mixture in the bottom of the prepared tin, cover with half the strawberries and remaining sponge fingers. Cover with a second third of the almond mixture, then the remaining strawberries and sponge fingers and finally the last of the almond mixture. Spread a piece of buttered greaseproof paper over the top, cover with a small plate and place a heavy weight on top to press it down. Put in the fridge and chill for at least 4 hours or overnight until the mixture is quite firm. To serve, invert the cake tin on to a serving plate and remove the tin. Decorate with whipped cream and strawberries.

Winter Buffet

MENUE

Smoked Mackerel Pâté
Individual Beef Wellingtons
Mixed Winter Salad
Cauliflower Cheese Salad
Prune and Orange Mousse
American Cranberry Flan

[Serves 12]

A hot dish for the main course of a winter buffet party gives everyone a feeling they are warm and well-fed; as the meat is cut into manageable chunks, these individual Beef Wellingtons are not difficult to eat just with a fork. Rather than using an expensive piece of steak for the filling, I have used a good-quality braising steak which is cooked slowly in a very little liquor until it is quite tender; the cooked meat is then put into the pastry with a mushroom and pâté stuffing. They can be cooked in advance and reheated, although they are at their best when freshly baked; as they can be made up in advance and just kept in the fridge until you are ready to bake and serve them, this should not present too many problems. If you wish, once they have been baked you can reduce the oven temperature right down to 140 °C/275 °F., Gas Mark 1, and keep them warm for 30 minutes.

Smoked mackerel make an excellent pâté, which is very quick to make in a blender or food processor. The addition of some curd cheese, as well as butter, prevents it from being too rich and remember to season it very well with plenty of freshly milled black pepper. Serve with hot toast, or slices of French or wholemeal bread, which is slightly easier as it reduces the amount of work you have to do just before serving. At this time of year green salad stuff, such as lettuces, cucumber, tomatoes, etc. is always very expensive and often of poor quality, but you can make excellent salads from some of the root vegetables, such as carrots, and celeriac. In the Mixed Winter Salad they have been combined with finely shredded Dutch or white cabbage, with a very little finely sliced red pepper for added colour, all tossed in French dressing just before serving. The Cauliflower Cheese

Salad uses raw cauliflower marinated in a mayonnaise and cheese sauce, and this rather piquant salad goes very well with the Beef Wellingtons.

Cranberries add a beautiful touch of colour to winter meals, but when served as a dessert they need to be teamed up with something fairly sweet to counteract their rather bitter taste. This American flan with a biscuit crumb base and filling of condensed milk, cream and lemon rind and juice is not dissimilar to a cheesecake, and the flavours blend extremely well together. It is very sad that so many people are put off prunes for life by school prunes and custard, as prunes can be turned into delicious desserts such as this Prune and Orange Mousse and are far from scorned in Continental cookery.

Work Plan

The day before
★ Make Smoked Mackerel Pâté, cover and keep in fridge until ready to serve.
★ Cook beef for Beef Wellingtons.
★ Make Prune and Orange Mousse.

In the afternoon
★ Put Mateus Rosé into fridge to chill.
★ Prepare Beef Wellingtons, put on baking trays in fridge and cover until ready to bake.
★ Make Cauliflower Cheese Salad, cover and put in a cool place.
★ Prepare Mixed Winter Salad, cover and put in a cool place.
★ Make American Cranberry Flan and keep in fridge until ready to serve.
★ Turn out Prune and Orange Mousse and decorate; keep in fridge until ready to serve.
★ Garnish pâté, cover until ready to serve.

Before serving
★ Put Beef Wellingtons into oven 20 minutes before serving.
★ Slice bread or make toast for Smoked Mackerel Pâté.
★ Toss Mixed Winter Salad just before serving.

Smoked Mackerel Pâté

3 large smoked mackerel
225 g/8 oz. softened butter
350 g/12 oz. curd cheese
juice 1½ lemons
2 teaspoons dried dill
2–3 cloves garlic, crushed
salt and freshly milled black pepper

To garnish
cucumber slices

Skin and bone the mackerel, and either flake and mash
finely or put into a blender with the butter. Beat in all
the remaining ingredients, then taste and adjust the
seasoning. Turn into a serving dish and swirl up the top
to make an attractive pattern. Refrigerate for at least 12
hours for the flavours to infuse. Garnish with slices of
cucumber before serving with toast or French or
wholemeal bread.

Individual Beef Wellingtons

1.8 kg/4 lb. good-quality braising steak
2 tablespoons oil
2 large onions, peeled and finely chopped
1.5 dl/¼ pint Mateus Rosé
1.5 dl/¼ pint beef stock
salt and freshly milled black pepper
1 bouquet garni
25 g/1 oz. butter
100 g/4 oz. mushrooms, very finely chopped or minced
225 g/8 oz. canned liver pâté or
good-quality liver sausage
2 tablespoons chopped parsley
2 × 370 g/13 oz. packets frozen puff pastry, thawed
1 egg yolk
1 tablespoon water

Cut the meat into 3.5 cm/1½ inch cubes. Heat the oil in
a pan and fry one of the onions for 5 minutes. Add the
meat and fry on all sides until browned. Add the wine,
stock, seasoning and bouquet garni. Cover the pan and
simmer very gently for 1½ hours or until the meat is very
tender. Remove from the heat and allow to become quite
cold. Heat the butter in a small pan and fry the remaining onion for 5 minutes. Add the mushrooms and fry for

a further 5 minutes, then remove from the heat. Mash the liver pâté or liver sausage, and add to the mushrooms and onion with the parsley, seasoning and 3 tablespoons of the cooking liquor from the meat.

Roll out the pastry and cut into 12 rectangles, each 20 × 12.5 cm/8 × 5 inches. Divide the liver mixture between the pieces of pastry and spread neatly to within 2 cm/¾ inch of the edge. Divide the meat between the pieces of pastry, arranging in an even line down the centre. Blend the egg yolk with the water, brush the edges of the pastry with beaten egg and bring up the edges of each one so that the meat is completely enclosed. Place on a baking tray and brush all over with beaten egg. Roll out the pastry trimmings and cut into leaves to decorate the top. Place these in position and brush with egg. Place the baking trays in the fridge until required. Cook in a hot oven, 220 °C/425 °F., Gas Mark 7, for 20 minutes or until the pastry is golden brown.

Mixed Winter Salad

Finely shred 450 g/1 lb. white cabbage, and peel and grate 450 g/1 lb. carrots, 450 g/1 lb. celeriac and a medium-sized onion. Finely slice a small red pepper, discarding the core and seeds. Put all the vegetables into a serving bowl with 2 tablespoons chopped parsley and mix lightly. Pour over 6 tablespoons French dressing just before serving and toss well.

Cauliflower Cheese Salad

Break a large cauliflower into florets, wash and dry thoroughly. Blend 3 dl/½ pint mayonnaise with 150 g/ 6 oz. finely grated Cheddar cheese and 2 teaspoons English mustard. Add the cauliflower, mix well, then turn into a serving dish, cover and chill for at least 4 hours. Turn into a serving dish and sprinkle with the paprika before serving.

Prune and Orange Mousse

225 g/8 oz. prunes
grated rind and juice 2 oranges
3 dl/½ pint water plus 4 tablespoons
75 g/3 oz. sugar
15 g/½ oz. powdered gelatine
2 egg whites
1.5 dl/¼ pint single cream
1.5 dl/¼ pint double cream

To decorate
1 orange, sliced

Soak the prunes for 6 hours or overnight in the orange juice and 3 dl/½ pint water. Put into a pan, together with the soaking liquor, orange rind and sugar. Cover and simmer very gently for about 30 minutes or until the prunes are very tender. Drain the prunes, reserving the cooking liquor, and make this up to 3 dl/½ pint with water if necessary. Stone the prunes, and sieve or purée in a blender together with the cooking liquor and orange rind. Sprinkle the gelatine over the remaining 4 tablespoons cold water in a basin. Leave to soften for 5 minutes, then stand the basin over a pan of hot water and leave until the mixture has dissolved; then stir carefully into the prune purée and allow to cool, but not set. Whip the double and single cream together until thick; put half on one side for decorating, then fold the remainder into the prune purée. Whisk the egg whites until they form stiff peaks, then fold these into the prune mixture. Turn into a 1.2 litre/2 pint mould, put into the fridge and leave for at least 4 hours or until set. To turn out, dip the mould quickly in hot water then invert on to a plate. Decorate with the reserved whipped cream and orange slices.

American Cranberry Flan

125 g/5 oz. digestive biscuits
50 g/2 oz. butter
25 g/1 oz. soft brown sugar
290 g/10½ oz. can condensed milk
grated rind and juice 2 lemons
1.5 dl/¼ pint single cream
225 g/8 oz. cranberries
50 g/2 oz. granulated sugar
4 tablespoons water

Crush the digestive biscuits. Melt the butter in a pan, remove from the heat and stir in the sugar and biscuits. Press into a 20 cm/8 inch fluted flan ring on a baking tray or loose-bottomed flan tin and chill. Pour the milk into a bowl and stir in the lemon rind and juice and the cream. Turn into the flan case and spread the filling evenly. Put into the fridge and leave for 1 hour. Put the cranberries into a pan with the granulated sugar and water and poach gently for 5 minutes or until soft. Remove from the heat and allow to cool. When the cranberries are quite cold, spoon carefully over the top of the lemon mixture and chill for at least a further 30 minutes. Remove the flan ring or tin before serving and place on a serving dish.

PART FIVE

OUTDOOR EATING

One of the delights of summer is being able to eat out of doors, whether it is a patio-type meal, such as the Summer Sunday lunch on page 14, a Summer Buffet as the one on page 46, a picnic or barbecue. In this chapter there is a menu for a Special Occasion Picnic, another, less elaborate, Family Picnic as well as a lunch-time and evening barbecue.

The secret of successful picnics is organization — before you leave home make quite sure that you have everything you need, such as salt and pepper, table napkins, a corkscrew, and, if you are rather forgetful like me, write yourself a check-list and tick off everything as you pack it up.

A large picnic basket and cool box are, of course, the ideal equipment, but the fact that you don't possess either should not stop you from attempting an elegant picnic. Cutlery is no problem as you can use your normal home cutlery, but remember to take some polythene bags or plastic boxes to put the dirty ones in. If you don't have any suitable plates, paper ones are fine, but try to buy fairly stiff ones, as the cheaper kinds are inclined to bend and collapse if you put very much on them. Other essential, or useful bits and pieces to take are hot water in a thermos and some instant coffee (better than making the coffee at home and then letting it stew away for hours which makes it very bitter), milk, sugar and cups, a large roll of kitchen paper, table napkins, damp J-cloths in a polythene bag to wipe anything sticky, some cling-wrap to help wrap up any leftovers, salt and pepper and, of course, glasses for the wine and a corkscrew.

If you are having a lunch-time picnic it is advisable to put the Mateus Rosé into the fridge the night before and then, before you leave home, put the bottle or bottles into a large, strong polythene bag with plenty of ice. Close the bag and stand it in a plastic bucket or washing up bowl, just in case it starts to leak when the ice melts. Depending on how much ice you have used, the heat of the day, etc., the wine should keep well chilled for 2–3 hours.

Barbecues are a very relaxed way to entertain and, provided the meat is cooked slowly over the barbecue (so you don't end up with a charred outside and a raw inside), there is nothing to beat the flavour. One of the most common mistakes people make when barbecuing is not lighting the fire early enough. Charcoal takes a while to become really hot, and ideally you should not start cooking until it has become quite grey and this can take anything from 30 to 45 minutes, according to the size of the barbecue, how much charcoal you have used, how adept you are at lighting it, and even how much wind there is.

When lighting the barbecue use either a fire lighter or some of the special barbecue lighter jelly available. Never use methylated spirits either to light the fire, or pour it on at a later stage as it ignites instantly and can cause serious accidents. Always keep a small jug or water spray beside the barbecue so that you can damp the fire down a little if it becomes too fierce. When you have finished cooking, douse the fire with water and make sure it is thoroughly extinguished. Any charcoal that is left unburnt can be spread out and left to dry so that it can be re-used another time.

Although I have given desserts for both these menus it can be fun to barbecue fruits over the dying embers. Bananas respond particularly well to this treatment and are best cooked in their skins and then served hot with whipped cream or ice cream, with a sprinkling of rum or liqueur if wished. Other fruits, such as pineapple, oranges, apples and grapefruit can all be cut into thick slices and cooked over the fire. You can either sprinkle them with a little brown sugar before cooking, or brush them with some golden or maple syrup before and during cooking.

Should it rain, both the meat dishes can be cooked very successfully under the grill. They will not have quite the same flavour, but at least some poor person is not left outside manfully trying to shield both the barbecue and himself from the wet with a large umbrella, and trying to cook the food at the same time!

Special Occasion Picnic

MENU

Pâté with Jellied Consommé
Seafood Flan
Green Potato Salad
Peperonata Salad
Tossed Green Salad
Strawberry Meringue Layer

[Serves 6]

Providing the weather is kind to you, there are few things more luxurious than drinking good wine and eating good food on a picnic, whether it is at lunch-time or on a long summer evening. Such picnics are also very relaxing for the hostess, as once you have left home it is impossible for you to have last-minute panics and all you have to do is serve up the food.

The French are particularly fond of small items, such as pâté and other charcuterie and hard or soft-boiled eggs set in jellied consommé. Although consommé will set on its own I have added a very small amount of gelatine here as if the weather is warm it could melt before you want to eat it. A seafood flan of prawns and crab, with plenty of chopped parsley to give it colour, tastes as good as it looks, and is very easy to transport in a china flan dish, such as the one in the picture. It is important not to over-cook this flan; not only does this spoil the egg custard as with any other flan, but over-cooking also toughens the prawns, so only cook it until it is just set, and allow it to become quite cold before putting in the fridge.

There are a good variety of salads to go with the flan, without involving too many different carrying containers, and the only salad which requires a separate dressing to be added at the last moment is the Tossed Green Salad and fresh herbs added to a green salad improve it enormously.

The Strawberry Meringue Layer can be made in any bowl, preferably unbreakable just to be on the safe side. The dessert itself will, however, withstand quite a bit of bumping about without being ruined and if it is prepared several hours before serving the juices from the strawberries just start to soften the meringue which gives it a very pleasant texture.

56

Pâté with Jellied Consommé

6 fresh or frozen asparagus spears
salt
150 g/6 oz. pork pâté or terrine
1 teaspoon powdered gelatine
425 g/15 oz. can consommé
2 tablespoons Mateus Rosé

Cook the asparagus in boiling salted water until just tender. Drain well, reserving the cooking liquor. Cut off the tips of the asparagus and reserve. Chop the remainder and divide between 6 small ramekin dishes. Cut the pâté into 6 pieces, place a piece in each dish and top with the reserved asparagus points. Pour off 2 tablespoons of the asparagus liquor into a cup, allow to cool, then sprinkle over the gelatine and leave to soften for 5 minutes. Stand the cup in a pan of gently simmering water and allow to dissolve. Gently heat the can of consommé just so that it is quite liquid, add the gelatine and the Mateus Rosé and stir well. Pour over the pâté in the dishes, then put into the fridge and leave until set.

Seafood Flan

For the pastry
225 g/8 oz. flour
pinch salt
100 g/4 oz. butter or margarine
about 2 tablespoons water

For the filling
25 g/1 oz. butter
1 medium-sized onion, peeled and chopped
3 eggs
3 dl/½ pint single cream
2 tablespoons chopped parsley
100 g/4 oz. shelled prawns
100 g/4 oz. crab meat – fresh, frozen or canned
a pinch of grated nutmeg
a pinch cayenne pepper
salt and freshly milled black pepper

Sift together the flour and salt. Rub in the butter until the mixture resembles fine breadcrumbs, then bind with the water to make a firm dough. Roll out and use to line a 22.5 cm/9 inch round flan dish or tin or an oval dish 17.5 × 27.5 cm/7 × 11 inches. Prick the base lightly with a fork, fill the centre with a circle of greaseproof paper and some baking beans, and bake in a moderately hot oven, 200 °C/400 °F., Gas Mark 6, for 10 minutes. Remove the greaseproof paper and beans, and bake for a further 5 minutes to dry out the base. Reduce the oven temperature to 180 °C/350 °F., Gas Mark 4. Melt the butter in a small pan, add the onion and fry gently for 5 minutes. Beat the eggs, then beat in the cream. Add the fried onion, parsley, prawns, and crab meat, together with any liquid from frozen or canned fish. Season with nutmeg, cayenne pepper and plenty of salt and freshly milled black pepper. Pour into the flan case and bake in a moderate oven for 30–40 minutes or until the mixture is just set. Remove from the oven and allow to cool, then refrigerate until leaving for the picnic.

Variation: Use a small bunch of chopped spring onions in place of the ordinary onion and replace the crabmeat with cooked, flaked smoked haddock.

Work Plan

The day before

★ Put Mateus Rosé into fridge to chill.
★ Make Pâté with Jellied Consommé.
★ Make Seafood Flan.
★ Make Green Potato Salad.
★ Make Peperonata Salad.
★ Make meringues for Strawberry Meringue Layer.
★ Make dressing for Tossed Green Salad.

In the morning

★ Assemble Strawberry Meringue Layer.
★ Prepare Tossed Green Salad.

Green Potato Salad

Scrub 450 g/1 lb. new potatoes and cook in boiling salted water until just tender. Drain and allow to cool, then either peel the potatoes or leave the skins on and cut into halves or quarters, depending on their size. Blend 4 tablespoons mayonnaise with 2 tablespoons soured cream. Add to the potatoes with ½ bunch finely chopped watercress, 2 tablespoons chopped parsley and 4 finely chopped spring onions. Mix well together and season to taste with salt and freshly milled black pepper, then pack into a suitable container.

Peperonata Salad

Cut 2 green and 2 red peppers into rings, discarding the cores and seeds. Heat 2 tablespoons olive oil in a pan and gently fry the peppers with a crushed clove of garlic in a covered pan for 15 minutes. Remove from the heat and allow to cool, then add 1 tablespoon lemon juice, season to taste with salt and pepper, and pack into a suitable container.

Tossed Green Salad

Wash a large lettuce, ideally use a crisp one such as a cos, Iceberg or Webb's Wonder. Dry thoroughly and put into a container with ¼ sliced cucumber, a teaspoon chopped mint, a tablespoon chopped chives and a little fresh tarragon and basil, if available. Cover and keep in the fridge until ready to leave. Take some French dressing separately in a screw-topped container. Pour over about 3 tablespoons just before serving and toss lightly together.

Strawberry Meringue Layer

3 egg whites
150 g/6 oz. caster sugar plus 1 extra tablespoon
450–650 g/1–1½ lb. strawberries
1.5 dl/¼ pint double cream
1.5 dl/¼ pint single cream

Whisk the egg whites until they form stiff peaks. If using an electric beater gradually beat in the 150 g/6 oz. caster sugar a teaspoon at a time; if beating by hand, whisk in half the sugar a teaspoon at a time, then fold in the remainder. Pipe or pile in spoonfuls on to a baking tray lined with greased greaseproof or silicone paper. Bake in a very cool oven, 110 °C/225 °F., Gas Mark ¼, for about 2 hours or until crisp, then roughly crush most of the meringues, reserving a few for decorating. Slice most of the strawberries, reserving a few for decorating and sprinkle with the remaining tablespoon of sugar. Whisk the single and double cream together until stiff. Put a layer of strawberries in the bottom of a serving dish, spread with a layer of cream and top with crushed meringue. Repeat these layers, ending with a layer of cream, then decorate the top of the dish with the reserved strawberries and whole pieces of meringue.

Variation: Use 6 dl/1 pint passion fruit pulp in place of the strawberries. Fold into the cream, then layer as above. Finish with meringue.

Family Picnic

<U>

MENU

Devilled Chicken Drumsticks
Super Salad Baps
Glazed Gooseberry Tarts

[Serves 4]

A simple picnic for which you do not require any knives and forks as all the food is easy to eat with your fingers, but it is nonetheless a filling and interesting meal. Chicken drumsticks are extremely lean and because of this can become rather dry, which is why I have suggested roasting, rather than grilling them so that they remain moist and succulent. Allow them to cool in the roasting tin, then, when they are quite cold, put them on some kitchen paper to drain, before putting into a plastic box or wrapping in foil.

The Super Salad Baps are just soft baps filled with lettuce, tomato and green pepper, but in the middle there is a spoonful of soft cream cheese mixed with chives, which adds interest to the rolls, without making the lettuce go limp in the way it would if a dressing had been put on. If you wished you could also add some sliced cucumber as well and sprinkle the tomatoes with a little chopped fresh, or dried basil.

The Glazed Gooseberry Tarts are a sweet shortcrust pastry, baked blind in tartlet tins, then filled with cream, lightly poached goosberries and glazed with the thickened gooseberry syrup. Should you be unable to buy fresh gooseberries you could use frozen gooseberries or a 283 g/10 oz. can gooseberries instead.

Devilled Chicken Drumsticks

8 chicken drumsticks
40 g/1½ oz. butter
2 teaspoons made English mustard
1 tablespoon Worcestershire sauce
1 tablespoon tomato ketchup

Make several slits on each chicken drumstick about 0.5 cm/just under ¼ inch deep. Cream the butter, then gradually beat in the mustard, Worcestershire sauce and ketchup; you will find that not all these beat into the butter and you are left with a slightly curdled-looking mixture but this does not matter. Spread the mixture over the drumsticks, then lay them in a roasting tin. Roast in a moderately hot oven, 200 °C/400 °F., Gas Mark 6, for about 35 minutes, basting two or three times during cooking. Remove from the oven and allow to cool.

Super Salad Baps

4 soft baps
25 g/1 oz. butter
1 small lettuce
100 g/4 oz. light cream cheese
about 1 tablespoon milk
1 tablespoon chopped chives or spring onions
salt and freshly milled black pepper
2 large tomatoes
1 small green pepper

Cut the baps in half and butter the cut sides. Wash the lettuce and dry thoroughly, then divide between the bases of the baps. Beat the cream cheese with enough milk to give a soft, spreading consistency, then beat in the chives or spring onions, some salt and plenty of freshly milled black pepper. Put a spoonful of this in the centre of the lettuce. Slice the tomatoes and the pepper, discarding the core and seeds. Arrange on top of the lettuce, then cover with the tops of the baps. Wrap each roll separately in cling-wrap before placing in a large polythene bag or box.

Glazed Gooseberry Tarts

For the pastry
100 g/4 oz. plain flour
pinch salt
50 g/2 oz. butter
3 teaspoons caster sugar
1 egg yolk
about 2 teaspoons water

For the filling
225 g/8 oz. gooseberries
4 tablespoons water
50 g/2 oz. granulated sugar
5 tablespoons double cream
2 teaspoons arrowroot

Work Plan

The day before

★ **Put Mateus Rosé into fridge to chill.**
★ **Cook chicken drumsticks.**
★ **Make Glazed Gooseberry Tarts.**

In the morning

★ **Make Super Salad Baps.**

Sift together the flour and salt. Rub in the butter until the mixture resembles fine breadcrumbs, then add the sugar and bind with the egg yolk and a little water to form a stiff dough. Roll out and cut into eight 7.5 cm/ 3 inch circles. Use to line deep patty tins, prick the bases with a fork and bake in a moderate oven, 180 °C/ 350 °F., Gas Mark 4, for about 20 minutes or until pale golden brown. Remove from the oven, take out of the tins and allow to cool.

Put the gooseberries into a pan with the water and granulated sugar, and cook over a gentle heat for about 10 minutes or until the gooseberries are quite tender, but still whole. Allow to cool, then drain the gooseberries and make the liquid up to 1.5 dl/$\frac{1}{4}$ pint with water, if necessary. Blend 1 tablespoon of the gooseberry liquor with the arrowroot in a basin and bring the remainder to the boil in a small pan. Pour over the blended arrowroot, stirring, return the mixture to the heat and bring back to the boil, stirring all the time. Remove from the heat and allow to cool slightly, stirring frequently to prevent a skin from forming. Lightly whip the cream and divide between the tartlet cases. Arrange the gooseberries on top and spoon over the arrowroot glaze. Leave until the glaze has set, then pack into a tin or plastic box.

Barbecue Supper

MENU

Mixed Bean Salad
Garlic Bread
Spiced Pork Spare Ribs
Herbed Tomatoes
Baked Potatoes
Fresh Apricot Cheesecake

[Serves 6]

Spare rib pork chops are one of the best meats to barbecue as the marbling of the fat with the lean keeps the chops very moist, especially if you baste them regularly during cooking with the remains of the marinade. The easiest way to do this is with an old pastry brush (preferably a fairly thick one) which you can keep for this purpose. Although you could cook the jacket potatoes on the barbecue, they do take a very long time cooked this way and I think most people will find it easier to cook them in a hot oven, although they can be put on the barbecue for the last 15 minutes before serving to give them a slight 'charcoal' flavour. Some people wrap the potatoes in foil before baking, but as I think the nicest part of a jacket potato is the crisp skin I am not in favour of this method. Always remember to prick the potatoes before baking so that they do not burst in the oven or on the barbecue.

Dried beans make delicious salads and for the starter for this meal I have suggested combining white haricot and red kidney beans, which makes a very attractive salad. However you could use all one kind of bean, but do not use canned beans as the secret of a good bean salad is to toss the warm beans in the dressing so that they really absorb the flavour.

Fresh apricots make a very delicate cheesecake, and the ginger biscuits used in this recipe to make the base provide a very pleasant contrast of texture and flavour. This cheesecake freezes particularly well so you could make it up several days in advance if you wished, or you could make up two at the same time and freeze one for the winter to remind you of those pleasant summer days.

Mixed Bean Salad

100 g/4 oz. dried haricot beans
100 g/4 oz. red kidney beans
6 dl/1 pint stock
2 small onions
1 small bay leaf
4 tablespoons French dressing
3 sticks celery, chopped
1 green pepper, de-seeded and chopped
2 tablespoons chopped parsley
100 g/4 oz. garlic sausage, diced
salt and freshly milled black pepper

Soak the beans for at least 6 hours or overnight in cold water. Drain, put into a pan with the stock, one of the onions, peeled and the bay leaf. Bring to the boil, cover and simmer gently for 1–1½ hours or until quite tender. Drain, reserving the stock (this can be used as a base for a soup) and toss quickly in the French dressing and remaining onion, finely chopped, while still warm. Leave to cool, then add the celery, pepper, parsley and garlic sausage and toss lightly together. Taste and adjust the seasoning and pile into one large or individual serving dishes. Serve with garlic bread.

Work Plan

The day before
- ★ Soak beans overnight.

In the morning
- ★ Put Mateus Rosé into fridge to chill.
- ★ Put pork chops into marinade.
- ★ Cook beans.
- ★ Make Apricot Cheesecake.
- ★ Prepare Garlic Bread.

Before serving
- ★ Turn out cheesecake and decorate.
- ★ Complete bean salad.
- ★ Light barbecue 1 hour before serving.
- ★ Put potatoes into oven to bake 1 hour before serving.
- ★ Start cooking chops about 20 minutes before serving.
- ★ Put Garlic Bread on edge of barbecue 15 minutes before serving.
- ★ Put tomatoes on barbecue 5 minutes before serving.

Garlic Bread

Take a French stick and cut into slices, about 2.5 cm/ 1 inch thick, stopping short about 1.5 cm/½ inch from the base. Cream 50 g/2 oz. butter, and beat in a crushed clove garlic and plenty of freshly milled black pepper. Spread this butter on the slices of bread and wrap the loaf in foil. Put on the edge of the barbecue to heat through.

Spiced Pork Spare Ribs

6 spare rib pork chops
1 onion, peeled and finely chopped
3 cloves garlic, crushed
3 tablespoons soy sauce
1 tablespoon Worcestershire sauce
2 tablespoons black treacle
3 tablespoons oil
2 tablespoons cider vinegar
salt and freshly milled black pepper

Put the spare ribs into a shallow dish. Mix all the remaining ingredients together and pour over the chops. Cover and marinate in a cool place for at least 8 hours, turning and basting with the marinade from time to time. Remove from the marinade and grill over hot charcoal for about 20 minutes or until quite tender, turning and basting with the remains of the marinade from time to time.

Herbed Tomatoes

Cut 6 tomatoes in half. Season with salt and freshly milled black pepper and sprinkle with chopped fresh or mixed dried herbs. Place over the barbecue and cook for about 5 minutes.

Fresh Apricot Cheesecake

450 g/1 lb. fresh apricots
1.5 dl/¼ pint water
100 g/4 oz. granulated sugar
juice 1 orange
15 g/½ oz. powdered gelatine
225 g/8 oz. cottage cheese, sieved
1.5 dl/¼ pint double cream, lightly whipped
40 g/1½ oz. butter
100 g/4 oz. ginger biscuits, crushed
25 g/1 oz. soft brown sugar

To decorate
3 tablespoons apricot jam
1 tablespoon water
1 tablespoon flaked almonds

Halve and stone the apricots, and put into a pan with half the water, the sugar and orange juice. Cover and simmer for 20 minutes or until tender. Remove about 8 apricot halves for decorating and put on one side. Purée the remainder and allow to cool. Sprinkle the gelatine over the remainder of the water in a small basin and leave to soften for 5 minutes. Stand the basin over a pan of gently simmering water and leave until the gelatine has dissolved. Fold the apricot purée into the cottage cheese, then the gelatine and finally the whipped cream. Turn into a 17.5 cm/7 inch round, loose-bottomed cake tin and chill for at least 1 hour. Melt the butter in a small pan, remove from the heat and stir in the crushed biscuits and sugar. Mix well, then sprinkle over the cheesecake and press down lightly. Chill for at least a further 2–3 hours.

To serve the cheesecake, invert the tin on to a serving plate and remove. Arrange the reserved apricots on the top. Sieve the apricot jam into a small pan, add the water, then bring to the boil and boil rapidly for 2 minutes. Remove from the heat, allow to cool slightly, then brush this glaze all over the top of the cake. Leave to set then sprinkle with the flaked almonds.

Barbecue Lunch

MENU

Home-made Hamburgers
Tomato Salad with Basil
Fresh Orange Mille Feuilles

[Serves 8]

Work Plan

In the morning

★ Put Mateus Rosé into fridge to chill.
★ Make Fresh Orange Mille Feuilles.
★ Make hamburgers.
★ Slice tomatoes and place in serving dish.

Before serving

★ Light barbecue about 1 hour before serving.
★ Start cooking hamburgers about 15 minutes before serving.
★ Pour over dressing and toss salad 15 minutes before serving.

Home-Made Burgers

900 g/2 lb. good-quality lean minced beef
2 egg yolks
2 dill cucumbers, finely chopped
3 cloves garlic, crushed
1 medium-sized onion, peeled and grated
2 tablespoons Worcestershire sauce
2 teaspoons chopped fresh thyme
salt and freshly milled black pepper
8 soft rolls or baps
8 large lettuce leaves
1 large onion, peeled and sliced

Put the beef into a bowl with the egg yolks, cucumbers, garlic, grated onion, Worcestershire sauce, thyme and plenty of seasoning. Mix well together, then divide into 8 equal-sized pieces. Lightly flour your hands and form into 8 burgers slightly larger than the rolls, as they shrink on cooking. Cook the hamburgers for a minimum of 5 minutes on each side or for up to 10 minutes according to how well cooked you like them and the heat of the fire. Put each burger into a bap with a large lettuce leaf and a few onion rings.

Tomato Salad with Basil

Slice 900 g/2 lb. tomatoes and place in a salad bowl. Pour over 5 tablespoons French dressing and sprinkle with 2 teaspoons chopped fresh basil. Toss.

Fresh Orange Mille Feuilles

370 g/13 oz. packet frozen puff pastry, thawed
beaten egg to glaze
100 g/4 oz. unsalted butter
100 g/4 oz. icing sugar
100 g/4 oz. ground almonds
2 large oranges

Roll out the pastry and cut into two rectangles, about 15 × 35 cm/6 × 14 inches. Knock up the edges with the back of a knife, place on two baking trays and brush all over with beaten egg. Bake in a very hot oven, 230 °C/450 °F., Gas Mark 8, for about 12 minutes. Remove from the oven and allow to cool.

Cream the butter, beat in the icing sugar until light and fluffy, then beat in the ground almonds. Grate the orange rind, then peel the oranges, discarding all the white pith and cut into slices. Beat the orange rind into the butter mixture and spread this over one of the pieces of pastry. Cover with the sliced oranges and then the second slice of pastry. Dust with sifted icing sugar.

INDEX